Test of FAITH

Test of FAITH

Science and Christianity Unpacked

Edited by Ruth Bancewicz

www.testoffaith.com

15 14 13 12 11 10 09   7 6 5 4 3 2 1

This edition first published 2009 by Paternoster. Paternoster is an imprint of
Authentic Media
9 Holdom Avenue, Bletchley, Milton Keynes, Bucks, MK1 1QR, UK
1820 Jet Stream Drive, Colorado Springs, CO 80921, USA
Medchal Road, Jeedimetla Village, Secunderabad 500 055, A.P., India
www.authenticmedia.co.uk

Authentic Media is a division of Biblica UK, previously IBS-STL UK. Biblica UK is limited
by guarantee, with its registered office at Kingstown Broadway, Carlisle, Cumbria, CA3
0HA. Registered in England & Wales No. 1216232. Registered charity in England &
Wales No. 270162 and Scotland No. SCO40064.

British Library Cataloguing in Publication Data

A catalogue record for this book is available from the British Library

ISBN-13: 978-1-84227- 663-1

Unless otherwise stated, Scripture quotations are taken from the HOLY BIBLE, NEW
INTERNATIONAL VERSION. Copyright (c) 1973, 1978, 1984 by the International Bible
Society. Used by permission of Hodder & Stoughton Limited. All rights reserved. 'NIV' is
a registered trademark of the International Bible Society UK trademark number 1448790

Figure on page 91 taken from *Life in our Hands* by John Bryant and John Searle,
published by IVP 2004. Copyright © 2004 John Bryant and John Searle. Used with
Permission of IVP.

Pages 64-66 & 108 based on Creation or Evolution, *Do We Have to Choose?* By Denis
Alexander, published by Monarch Books. Used with permission of Lion Hudson plc.

Extract on page 91 taken from *Beyond Belief* by Denis Alexander and Robert S. White,
published by Lion 2004. Copyright © 2004 Denis Alexander and Robert S. White. Used
with permission of Lion Hudson plc.

Diagram on page 58 by Derek West, taken from *Beyond Belief* by Denis Alexander
and Robert S. White, published by Lion 2004. Copyright © 2004 Denis Alexander and
Robert S. White. Used with permission of Lion Hudson plc.

Pages 87-88 based on *Cloning Humans* by Denis Alexander, published by the Jubilee
Centre. Used with permission of the Jubilee Centre, **www.jubilee-centre.org**, Jubilee
House, 3 Hooper Street, Cambridge, CB1 2NZ

Page 109 based on *Global Warming, Climate Change and Sustainability: Challenge to
Scientists, Policymakers and Christians* by Sir John Houghton, published by the John
Ray Initiative 2007. Used with permission of the John Ray Initiative.

Page 110 based on *Climate Change Controversies: A Simple Guide* published by The
Royal Society, 2007. Used with permission of the Royal Society.

Cover design by Contrapositive
Print Management by Adare
Printed and bound in the UK by J. F. Print Ltd., Sparkford, Somerset

Contents

Acknowledgements

The documentary Test of Faith was made by Contrapositive New Media (**www.contrapositive.tv**). Contrapositive are also responsible for the **www.testoffaith.com** website and the design and layout of all the Test of Faith print materials. They dived wholeheartedly into this project, rapidly absorbed our endless piles of science-faith material and address books full of contacts, and produced a documentary that we think is informative, imaginative and extremely high quality. The key people were: Executive Producer/Director of Photography John Ford, Director Mark Brickman, Producer Louisa Spicer and Editor Neil Edwards.

We want to thank all the scientists and theologians who took part in the documentary: Dr Denis Alexander, Professor Katherine Blundell, Professor John Bryant, Rev Dr Alasdair Coles, Dr Francis Collins, Professor Simon Conway Morris, Dr William A. Dembski, Professor Peter Harrison, Sir John Houghton, Dr Ard Louis, Professor Alister McGrath, Professor Bill Newsome, Dr Cherith Fee Nordling, Paul Taylor, Rev Dr John Polkinghorne, Rev Dr David Wilkinson and Dr Jennifer Wiseman.

A number of people have been involved in an advisory or editorial capacity for the documentary or course: Lin Ball, Dr Zoë Binns, Professor John Bryant, Paul Butler, Dr Wayne Floyd, Dr Lisa Goddard, Dr Loren Haarsma, Dr Deborah Haarsma[i], Rev Dr Rodney Holder, Richard James, Dr Ard Louis, Dr Hilary Marlowe, Dr Rebecca McLaughlin, Dr Jonathan Moo, Dr Terry Morrison, Dr David Norman, Dr Jason Rampelt, Rev David Robertson, Rev Dominic Smart, Professor Robert White and Ro Willoughby. Stephen Chikazaza, Jamie Brown and Rowena Gee helped to choose the song list.

Almost twenty people organized groups to pilot the course, in the US and the UK: Dr Andrew Bowie, Dr Adrian Bowman, Bryonie Brodie, Professor Dan Burden, Jill Clark, Glen Davis, Perry Enever, Professor Darrel Falk, Dr Tom Heard, Dr Nicole Maturen, Rev Peter Milner, Rev Lyndon North, Clare Parkinson, Rev David Robertson, Dr Geoff Sackett, Professor Richard Schaeffer, Benjamin Shank, Dr Morven Shearer, Professor Joan Sotherden, Dr Keith Suckling, Professor David Vosburg, Dr Leslie Wickman and Professor Paul Wraight.

We would also like to express our gratitude to all the others who have been involved in this project in giving advice and support, or taking part in surveys. Thanks also go to Tara Smith and Robin Parry at Paternoster for their encouragement and patience in producing these materials.

The material does not necessarily represent the views of the people acknowledged here, and the editor takes responsibility for the final content.

Ruth Bancewicz, Editor

Quick-start Guide

We have designed this course so that leaders can run it with a minimum of preparation. Although leaders who make the time to prepare by looking through this guide carefully will get the most out of the course (as, therefore, will the rest of the group), we thought we'd better be realistic. Below are a few hints and tips for those who begin preparing half an hour before the session.

Before running the course:

- Read the one-page Documentary Summary on page 100.
- Look at the one-page Course Overview on page 10 and decide which sessions to use.
- Read the short list of Tips for Running a Good Course on page 13.
- Read as much of 'Introduction to the Course' on pages 8 and 9 as you can.
- Make sure you have enough copies of the *Study Guide* for everyone in the group, as well as some copies of the book *Test of Faith: Spiritual Journeys with Scientists*.

Before each session you will need to:

- Make sure you have the DVD and something to play it on.
- Look through the session notes and decide which introduction and epilogue activities might suit your group.
- Identify the relevant Briefing Sheets.
- Decide whether you will use the Short Questions or a general one after each DVD segment.
- Have a quick look at the Discussion Topics so you have an idea of how to guide the discussion.
- Make sure you have enough:
  - *Study Guides* for everyone.
  - Pens and Bibles – if people won't be bringing them.

We have designed the course so that anyone can run it and have provided all the scientific information that you need in the glossary and Briefing Sheets. If you don't have a science background yourself and want to save time in preparation you could invite a science graduate along to answer your questions.

www.testoffaith.com

Introduction to the Course

The aim of the *Test of Faith* materials is to help meet the enormous need in churches and parachurch groups for accessible materials on science and Christianity. The issues this course addresses have an impact on our faith and are relevant to life in the world today.

Why 'Test of Faith'? The challenge that has been put forward so many times recently is that God is a delusion and science has removed the need for faith in anything. How do believing scientists respond to this? They have all been trained to think and test ideas to the limit. If their faith and their science are both genuine searches for truth, we need to hear from them.

The main message that you should take away from the *Test of Faith* documentary is that there are many practising scientists who have a sincere Christian faith, even at the highest levels of academia. All of us can share their experience of awe when they find out more about God's creation through science. These scientists also help us to explore a number of issues that affect our own lives.

This course is designed to help you make the most of the documentary: to take any new concepts on board and then discuss them. The material is very much an introduction to science and Christianity. It may well provoke some questions that people didn't know that they had and open up some new areas of interest. There are many good books, articles and mp3s available to take things further, some of which are recommended in the Taking it Further lists for each session. There are also extra resources tailored specifically for the course on **www.testoffaith.com**.

The scientists interviewed on *Test of Faith* are all Christians. We have also interviewed some theologians, most of whom also have a scientific background. The book *Test of Faith: Spiritual Journeys with Scientists* tells the stories of ten of the scientists – their personal discovery of faith and how that has affected their work. It's a short book and an easy read. For many people this will be the most useful background reading for the course, so try to make a number of copies available for your group.

Christians hold different views on some of these issues. We're not expecting everyone to agree with all that the scientists and theologians say in the documentary. These are complex issues, and in the course material we have often laid out several different views that Christians take on a particular topic so that you can discuss them openly.

Most of all, *you do not have to be an expert* to run this course. In fact, being new to the subject can be an advantage, because you will be learning along with the group and are less likely to try to cover the material too quickly. We have provided all the scientific information that you need in the glossary and Briefing Sheets. For most of the questions we have given helps for the leader so that you can guide the discussion in a helpful direction and drop in hints if needed. If you don't have a science background yourself, and want to save time in preparation, you could invite a science graduate along to answer your questions.

Who is it for?

This course is designed primarily for small groups in an informal setting. It will also work well for larger groups that can break into smaller groups for discussion. Each session includes options for introduction and epilogue activities that will work for large groups (see guidelines for large groups on page 14).

We aim to bring the latest issues to churches and other groups in a number of settings – maybe at school, on campus, or at work. We've chosen a format that is flexible and user-friendly and have tried not to use scientific or theological jargon. These materials should be suitable for an audience of different ages, educational levels, learning types and faith backgrounds.

You do not have to be a scientist to be interested in science, and you definitely don't need any scientific knowledge to have Christian faith, but we hope that if people have the opportunity to think about science and faith together they will be able to engage with the scientific issues that have an impact on our faith, culture and practical aspects of our lives in a new way.

The main requirement for anyone taking part in the course is to be interested and open-minded. We have worked within a theological framework that is based on a high view of Scripture and in line with the major creeds of the Christian church. Where issues are secondary we have made that clear and laid out a range of views that Christians hold. Pastors from a number of different denominations have reviewed the materials.

Although the materials have been written for Christians, we have kept a second audience in mind: people who are interested in Christianity for a number of reasons and have questions about science and faith. Scientific issues often come up as Christians talk about their faith with their friends, so as well as being an excellent training tool for church members, the course has been designed to be used with mixed groups of Christians and others. So although the focus is on Christian faith, we have deliberately avoided Christian jargon and Scripture references in the documentary so that you can explore the biblical material at a suitable pace in the course (see page 14 for further details).

Our approach

The aim of each session's introduction is to help people see how the subject they will be tackling is relevant to them personally. This will be especially important for a group that is new to science-faith issues, and these activities will lead to livelier discussion later on in the session.

The documentary begins with questions that come from the world around us and proceeds to unpack them from a perspective of faith. Some people will relate to that initial feeling of conflict and want to work through that tension in the parts of the course that address it. Others may want to look at some of the specific issues raised at a deeper level, and they can use the bonus and/or in-depth sessions (see 'Course Overview', page 10) and the accompanying bonus DVD clips to do that.

After watching each episode of the documentary, general discussion or the optional Short Questions will allow people to digest the main points. Each discussion topic then brings out a key question from the documentary and allows the group to ask, 'What do you think?', 'Do you think these people are justified in what they are saying?' and 'What does the Bible have to say?'

These are issues that affect everyone at a deep level, and there are rarely easy 'black and white' answers. The Bible was written in a pre-scientific time and doesn't speak directly to all of the issues that new technologies and scientific ideas raise. There are always broader biblical principles that Christians can apply to any given situation, and so the course material brings those out where possible. These are subjects that have theologians and biblical scholars hard at work, so it's difficult to have a really in-depth discussion without a good deal more background knowledge. Having said that, everyone has to start somewhere and you do not need a degree in science or theology to understand the basics. This course will help people to find the answers where they do exist and to equip them for an informed discussion.

It's important to recognize that it is possible for Christians to hold different views on some issues. For example, where creation is concerned, the fact that God created the universe is vital, and the 'why' of that is important to all of us. The 'how' – the mechanism by which that happened – is a secondary issue, and as such it is open to discussion. The questions in every Discussion Topic will guide people in developing a broad understanding of the issue, but – especially towards the end of the topic – there are always some questions that will stimulate an open discussion and allow people to air their views.

The purpose of the epilogue activities is to help people process the things they have learned or discussed during the session – personally and spiritually, as well as intellectually. For some, this will be the most important part of the session and will help them to unwind and absorb what they have heard and remember it. Some sessions touch on issues that are personally challenging or sensitive, and here there are activities that deal with these issues on a more pastoral level using Bible passages, quotes from theologians and suggestions for prayer and reflection.

Taking it Further

The 'Taking it Further' sections will help people to keep on learning, but course leaders may want to do other things to address the questions that have been raised. Some members of the group may want to read one of the recommended books and come together again to discuss it. You may want to invite a speaker or arrange a series of talks with several churches in your area.

Finally, Christians in Science (UK) and the American Scientific Affiliation (USA) have regular conferences, and local groups are active in many different locations. There are similar groups in other parts of the world (see **www.testoffaith.com** for details).

Feedback

If you have feedback on how you found the course, and suggestions for improvements, do let us know. You can email us at **info@testoffaith.com** or write to:

Test of Faith
The Faraday Institute
St Edmund's College
Cambridge
CB3 0BN, UK

Ruth Bancewicz

Course Overview

Session 0

An optional introductory session for groups who want to spend time getting to know each other before running the course. The suggested activities will set the scene and get people talking.

Sessions 1 and 1b: Beyond Reason?

These sessions will get people interested in thinking about how science and Christian faith might speak to each other.

The Discussion Topics that Session 1 tackles include: Ways of relating science and faith; the Big Bang and how the universe looks as if it was 'fine-tuned' to be suitable for life; 'God of the gaps'; prayer and miracles. Session 1b is, overall, more personal and practical than Session 1. This session will help group members to explore the interface between science, or a scientific way of thinking, and their own faith.

Sessions 2 and 2b: An Accident in the Making?

Part 2 of the documentary looks briefly at several views on creation before moving on to examine critically the way that some Christians reconcile evolution with the Bible.

In addition to Session 2, an overview that addresses the main messages from *Test of Faith*, there are several optional in-depth sessions (2.1, 2.2 and 2.3) that look more deeply into the interpretation of Genesis, the science, and further questions on human evolution, the fall and suffering. Bonus Session 2b deals with the environment.

Sessions 3 and 3b: Is Anybody There?

Part 3 of the documentary examines who we are as human beings, made in the image of God.

Discussion topics include: 'the God spot'; 'an ethical toolkit'; and 'using your ethical toolkit: cloning'. Session 3b considers the image of God, the beginning of life, genetic testing, enhancement and 'emergence'.

Running the course

Equipment needed

- DVD, DVD player and TV/projector
- Pens and Bibles, if people won't be bringing them
- A *Study Guide* for each person if they don't already have one
- Depending on the options leaders choose for introductory activities, they will occasionally need to supply other materials. The leader's information section at the beginning of each session lists these items.
- You may want to bring along some copies of the books listed in the 'Taking it Further' sections at the end of each session for people to look at. If you are at a church that has a bookstall, you could ask them to stock some of the recommended books.

Extra resources available on the Test of Faith DVD

- A trailer for the *Test of Faith* documentary to show in a church service, for example, to advertise the course.
- Short videos, including five reflective pieces that you may find useful during the epilogue times; for example, to play while you read a Bible passage aloud, or use for a time of silent reflection.
- Subtitles in English, Chinese, Spanish, Portuguese, French and Russian. The soundtrack is also dubbed into Farsi, Turkish and Arabic.
- This disc contains additional resources, including poster and invitation templates and transcripts of the documentary and bonus clips that can be accessed by following these instructions:
  1. Open 'My Computer' on your PC, or 'Finder' on your Mac
  2. Right-click on the DVD disc labelled 'Test of FAITH' and select 'open'
  3. Open the directory/folder labelled 'Resources'

Many of these will also be available on the testoffaith.com website.

You will need Adobe Acrobat Reader or a similar application to open the PDF files (downloadable from **www.adobe.com)**.

Planning

Note: While it's not necessary for leaders to have watched the DVD through to the end before running the course, it will help in guiding the discussion.

Use the Course Overview (previous page) and the Documentary Summary (page 100) to help you decide which sessions to use.

Because one size never fits all for group studies, we have designed this course to be as flexible as possible. Each session runs for about 1 ½ – 2 hours. If you have a shorter or longer time available you can either leave out or add activities or discussion items.

There are four different emphases, or approaches, for each session. Choose the one that best suits the makeup of your group and the time you have available to meet:

Basic introduction	Dealing with the main ideas – nothing too technical (scientifically or theologically).
In-depth	Dealing with the main ideas, but in more depth.
Big picture	Focusing on broad ideas and principles rather than scientific details.
A group with a lot of scientific knowledge	For people who are comfortable with or interested in the scientific detail. This approach misses out the more basic scientific concepts and looks into issues that require a better understanding of the science.

The notes below also indicate the general difficulty level of each discussion topic. For an even more introductory session you may want to simply use the Short Questions to explore the main themes and the glossary and Briefing Sheets to explain any unfamiliar technical words and concepts.

Structure of each session

Preparation for Participants *(optional)*: These activities will help people think about why the session is relevant to their lives. Options include talking to friends, family members or colleagues, or reading or thinking about current affairs. We have found that this type of input makes the discussion during the session more lively because the issues really hit home.

Introduction *(10–15 minutes)*: These activities will help to break the ice and to reinforce the fact that these issues affect the people who are in the group and others that they know.

DVD and General Discussion / Short Questions *(45–60 minutes)*: The documentary episodes on the DVD are each 26–33 minutes long. We suggest watching each episode a chapter at a time, with a few minutes of discussion after each chapter (see notes below).

Discussion Topics *(25–30 minutes)*: There are several sets of questions to choose from for each session. For Bonus Sessions 1b, 2b and 3b there are shorter 'bonus clips' on the DVD to watch and Discussion Topics tailored to these clips.

Epilogue *(10–15 minutes)*: This time should help the overall message to sink in, encourage application and give time for quiet reflection and prayer. You may want to us the 'reflection' bonus videos during this time.

Taking it Further: At the end of each session there is a list of websites, online articles and books to explore. The website **www.testoffaith.com** also lists extra resources tailored specifically for the course.

DVD and General Discussion / Short Questions

Use the chapter menu to watch the relevant part of the documentary a chapter at a time. We have provided cues and time codes to show where to pause the DVD at the end of each chapter.

Hints:

- *You could read out the relevant Short Questions before you watch each chapter of the DVD, to let people know what to listen for. Some of the answers can be found on the relevant Briefing Sheet in Appendix 2.*

- *Use the Briefing Sheet for the episode you are watching as a recap if you need it.*

- *People shouldn't be worried about having a complete understanding of the more complex scientific concepts. The Discussion Topics that follow have been designed so that people who have an understanding of the general principle will be able to participate fully in the discussion.*

- *If your group members are more confident with science-faith issues or have been exposed to a number of these topics before, you may want to play the whole documentary episode through and spend some time discussing it generally before moving on to the more in-depth questions.*

- *Hearing the topics that interest people the most should help you to choose which Discussion Topics to tackle, or which of the bonus sessions to run later.*

Using the leader's notes

Though they are not answers, the notes in italics are there to help you guide the discussion if people have difficulty answering the question.

The Bible passages in the study notes are, in context, representative of overall biblical themes. In some instances you, or others in the group, may be able to think of different passages that will illustrate the point equally well.

The questions sometimes refer to the Briefing Sheets, but the main aim is for them to be introductory background information to help you to prepare, or for people to read before or after the session.

So that you can help the group to navigate through their course guides, we have indicated which page in the leaders guide corresponds to which page in the study guide. This has been marked on the top outside corner of the relevant pages of the leaders guide.

Tips for Running a Good Course

Almost twenty groups in the US and the UK piloted a draft version of this course, and we have gleaned some tips from the feedback that we received:

It is much more difficult to cultivate discussion in a larger group, and those with less scientific knowledge may be left behind. Fewer than 12 people is ideal, or split into smaller groups for the discussion times – with a leader for each one.

Do use the Introduction so that people can discover for themselves that these are issues that affect us all.

Don't be tempted to miss out the Epilogue. This is especially relevant for Session 1, where this is the main biblical content for the session.

Do take time to look through this leader's guide before you start the course, because the group will undoubtedly raise questions that are addressed in future sessions.

Don't overestimate people's prior knowledge of science or theology – give plenty of time for people to talk through the things they don't understand.

Do encourage people to do the preparation activities and some background reading – it will make the discussion times much livelier.

Don't try to use everything – less is more. Run multiple sessions rather than packing too much into one.

Do try to find a science graduate to help you with the scientific background. We have provided all the background information that you need, but having a handy expert around is always useful.

Don't worry about having all the answers – you are there to guide your group through the material, but in the *Study Guide* everyone has access to the same Briefing Sheets and 'Taking it Further' lists, so you can learn together.

Do try to keep a balance in the discussion between the 'experts' (giving them time to share and explain) and those who have less background knowledge (making sure they have equal opportunities to discuss and ask questions).

Do have copies of the book *Test of Faith: Spiritual Journeys with Scientists* available, because people will be interested in the stories of the life and faith of the scientists interviewed in the documentary.

Alternative Ways of Running the Course

- Spread each session over two weeks, and cover the material in more depth.
- Run a four- or five-session course, and pick the bonus and/or in-depth sessions that would be of most interest for your group.
- Run Sessions 1, 2 and 3, and then get the group to decide what other session(s) they would like to tackle.
- Run Sessions 1, 2 and 3 first using the Short Questions. Then offer further sessions for those who want to go over things again in more depth, using the Discussion Topics from the sessions you've done and/or the other bonus and in-depth sessions the group would like to tackle.
- Run Sessions 1, 2 and 3 and meet every two weeks, offering bonus and in-depth sessions as an optional extra in the intervening weeks.
- Schedule the sessions to meet more than one week apart, to allow time for extra reading in between. You could decide as a group what you will read to follow up the last session and/or to prepare for the next one.
- If you are doing Sessions 1, 2 and 3 only, you could use some questions from the bonus and in-depth sessions.
- For Bonus Sessions 1b and 3b you may also wish to add a Discussion Topic that you did not tackle in Session 1 or 3.

Not just for Christians

Science-faith issues often get people talking, regardless of their faith background. The design of the course is such that it is suitable for groups of people who may not all be Christians but who are interested in talking about science-faith issues within a Christian context.

- Each session includes introduction and epilogue activities that don't assume any particular beliefs. Many of the other activities can be used for a 'debrief' without prayer, if that's more appropriate in your group.
- The questions on faith issues usually ask, 'What do Christians believe?' or 'What does the Bible passage say?' rather than assuming that the participants are Christians. The rest of the questions are relevant for everyone, regardless of their beliefs.
- Finally, Bonus Session 1b gives the most opportunities for people to talk about their own views on faith. You may want to use one or two of the questions from this session instead of the Discussion Topics for Session 1.

Guidelines for large groups

While this course was designed with small groups in mind, it can be adapted for a larger group:

- Some of the Introduction activities are designed for large groups.
- You will need to break into groups of less than 12 for discussion and assign a leader, who will prepare in advance, for each group.
- You will need to watch the DVD as a large group and split into smaller groups for discussion. If you have a scientist helping you, you may want to go through the Short Questions or have some general discussion first, before breaking into smaller groups for the Discussion Topics.
- Alternatively, you could have one small group per Discussion Topic, so that people can choose which topic they would like to investigate further.

Session 0: Introduction

Aim of the session

This is an optional introductory session for groups who want to spend some time getting to know each other before running the course. We have suggested some activities that will set the scene and get people talking. Do be open yourself about your experience of science and faith and the questions that you have, and encourage the group to do the same.

If you are meeting in the evening you may want to eat together before you start.

Mix and match the suggestions for the session below as appropriate.

Introduction

- Have something around the room for people to do as they arrive. Use one of the introductory activities for this: Session 1 Option 4, or Session 1b Option 1.
- Pray to start the session – you could either read a Psalm (try Psalm 8 or 19) and pray from the front, or if people have just come in from a busy day, have a time of silence and close in prayer.
- Get people to introduce themselves. As part of their introduction ask everyone to answer one or more of:
  - Why did you come? What do you hope to get out of the course?
  - Which question or topic are you most hoping to address in this course? *Make a note of these and use them to help you in your preparation of future sessions.
  - What things have you enjoyed that have to do with science? (E.g., an inspiring science teacher at school, nature documentaries on TV, using the latest technology, finding out how things work, etc.)
  - Has science ever made you think about God? If so, how?

Discussion

- Show the trailer for the documentary.
- Ask one of these questions:
  - What are the questions that it raises for you?
  - What are the most interesting questions to do with science and faith that you have come across?
  - What are the most important messages in the trailer?
  - How relevant to your own life are the questions that the trailer raises?
  - Have you come across anything in the media about science and faith recently?
- You could also use one of the other introductory activities from Session 1.

Epilogue

- Use one of the Epilogue Options from Session 1.
- Pray in pairs or small groups for the course.

Session 1: Beyond Reason? Science, Faith and the Universe

Planning

Aim

Science and faith are important in areas that affect all of us, including education ('Why aren't there dinosaurs in the Bible daddy?'), medicine ('*Should* we use this new technology?'), and politics ('Why are we being told to be "green"? Surely the world has got to end at some point anyway?')

This session will set the scene and get people interested in thinking about how science and Christian faith might speak to each other before they move on to thinking about more practical issues later in the course. What people learn in this session should affect the way they think and react in conversation with friends, family and colleagues, and also how they relate to current events. The optional preparation and introductory activities will help those who have never really considered these issues to realize that they are relevant to them personally.

The first part of the documentary should leave the viewer with three main messages:

- It is possible to be a scientist and a Christian, even at the highest levels of academia.
- The world is an incredible place. Science is a way of learning more about God through understanding what he has created.
- Astronomy raises some interesting questions about God. These questions are a good example of how science and faith can speak to each other.

The discussion time is an opportunity to unpack several of the issues that the documentary raises in more detail, and especially:

- Ways of relating science and faith
- The Big Bang, and how the universe looks as if it was 'fine-tuned' to be suitable for life
- 'God of the gaps'
- Prayer and miracles.

Note: This part of the documentary looks at the Big Bang and a universe that is billions of years old. For some this may be new or controversial, but our aim is to engage with 'mainstream' science – what are these scientists, who are Christians, encountering every day in their research? How could we think about these issues as Christians? The course material does not mention Genesis here because Session 2 will deal with it in depth, so try to defer questions on the age of the universe until then. Even if the jury is out for your group on how to interpret Genesis, it is important to know how Christians working in science are dealing with these issues in the light of their faith. The focus should be, as much as possible, on the many insights in this section that are not related to the actual timescale of creation.

Equipment needed

- If using Introduction Option 4 for a large group, photocopy Sheet 1 or 2 and bring post-it notes and Blu-Tack.
- You may want a flip chart or sheets of paper if using Epilogue Option 2.

There are four Briefing Sheets for this session. The session notes refer to three of these, and 'Scientists and Faith through History' is extra reading for those who are interested.

Some suggestions for a 1 ½ – 2 hour session:

	Basic introduction	In-depth	Big picture	A group with a lot of scientific knowledge
Introduction Option	1	4	2	3
DVD	✓	✓	✓	✓
Ch. 1: How Do People See the World?		✓	✓	✓
Ch. 2: The Big Bang / God of the Gaps? / Miracles	✓			
Ch. 3: The Anthropic Principle		✓		✓
Ch. 4: How Do You View Science and Faith?			✓	
Recap	✓			
Epilogue Option	any	1	3	2

To split into two shorter sessions *(40–60 minutes each)*

Ask the group to read the material related to this session in the *Study Guide* beforehand.

First half-session:

- Introduction activity in pairs *(5 minutes)*
- DVD – watch and discuss for 5 minutes after each chapter – you may only get through the first two or three chapters in the first half-session
- Epilogue *(5 minutes)*

Second half-session:

- Quick recap by leader *(5 minutes)*
- Finish watching DVD if needed
- Discussion Topics – pick one or two that raised the most interest, or split into smaller groups to discuss different topics
- Epilogue *(5 minutes)*

Preparation for Participants *(optional):*
Why bother thinking about science and faith?

The aim is to help people to realize that science and faith do come up in the media and science-faith issues do affect their lives. People could do either of these two exercises, and when you come to the session the most relevant introductory activity would be Option 2 or 4 – or you could just generally discuss what people found out.

Of course, if this is your first session and you want to use one of these activities, you will need to contact the group at least a week in advance.

Ask two or three friends, family members or colleagues if they can think of a situation where science and religion (or beliefs) affect each other. What issues or questions arise?

For example, what about:

- In medicine? (Religious beliefs often affect ethical decisions.)
- In education? (Children sometimes ask questions like 'Who made human beings, God or evolution?')
- In politics? (E.g., the Archbishop of Canterbury is campaigning on climate change.)

or

When you watch TV, listen to the radio, or read the paper, keep an eye out for stories that mention both science and faith. What issues or questions arise? What effect do these issues have on society?

Introduction *(10–15 minutes)*

This section will set the scene for the course and, most importantly, will help people to realize how these issues are relevant to their own lives.

Note: Option 1 is related to the questions addressed in the documentary and will help a group to take in what is said more easily – especially if they are completely new to this topic.

Option 1: True or False

Here's a series of statements about the issues that the documentary will tackle. Read them out and ask people to say or make a note if they think each statement is true or false, or if they are not sure (our answers are written in the 'Recap' section on page 25). If you want this to be more active, you could allocate three different places in the room as 'true', 'false' and 'not sure' and ask people to move to the appropriate place to answer.

Q1: Science and faith are at war

Q2: There are some conflicts between science and faith

Q3: Most of the first scientists in history were Christians

Q4: When science can't explain something, that is evidence for the existence of God

Q5: When science *can* explain something, you see evidence for God

Q6: Science and faith are two different ways of looking at the same world

Q7: Some questions cannot be answered by science

Q8: If the universe started with a Big Bang, God lit the 'blue touch paper' (the fuse)

Q9: Some scientists think there are many universes

Q10: Understanding more about nature will help us to learn more about God

Option 2: Sharing Experiences

Q: When in the past have you been challenged to think about science and faith? What did you learn?

For example:
- A conversation with a friend who claimed that science has disproved the existence of God
- An incident in the classroom, lecture hall or workplace
- A TV programme, book or newspaper article

Option 3: How do you view science and faith?

Use the Discussion Topic for DVD Chapter 4 (page 24) to talk about what people think of the relationship between science and faith. You could either discuss your views openly as a group or ask people to hand in slips of paper (anonymously) with their particular views and present the results in a suitable way. It should be useful and interesting to do this exercise at the beginning of the course, and you could revisit it again at the end of the course to see if people's ideas have changed at all.

Option 4: Have you heard this?

Use the list of quotes on Sheet 1 or 2 (pages 28-30). Has anyone heard something like this before? (Perhaps not the exact quote, but something like it?) Have they thought about any of these things themselves? The idea is to jog people's memories and help them to realize that these issues do affect them. Give people time to say how they felt before moving on to the documentary and addressing the issues directly.

- You could photocopy the sheet, cut each quote out, and discuss them in turn.
- Or you could spread them out and let people choose one that they have heard before.
- For a larger group you could enlarge them, cut them out and stick them around the walls with Blu-Tack, and use post-it notes or markers for people to indicate which ones they have heard before.

Watch *Test of Faith* Part 1: Beyond Reason? *(45–60 minutes)*

Use the chapter menu to watch Part 1 of the documentary a chapter at a time. Pause the DVD at the end of each chapter using the cues below (press pause after you hear the cue).

Chapter 1 – John Polkinghorne: '… really rich and remarkable world in which we live.' [Time code: 7 min. 41]
Chapter 2 – Katherine Blundell: '… and this is a practice known as God of the Gaps, and it's dangerous.' [Time code: 14 min. 00]
Chapter 3 – Alister McGrath: '… there's a correspondence between the theory and the observation.' [Time code: 18 min. 54]
Chapter 4 – Jennifer Wiseman: '… exploration is a divinely Christian activity and people should be excited about it.'
[Time code: 25 min. 47]

Note: The last chapter of Part 1 is the trailer for Part 2, so you could play it at the end of the session to inspire people to come again.

After each chapter take a few minutes (depending on the size of your group) to help people process what they have just seen. For general discussion use an open question such as:

- What was new or most interesting for you?
- What did you find most surprising or challenging?
- What do you think the main messages were?
- What do you think? Do you agree?

Or you could use the Short Questions below.

Short Questions:

Chapter 1

Q: Why do people today sometimes think that there is a conflict between science and religion?

A: Partly because of the work of Huxley and others who wanted to give science a higher profile and take it away from the clergy, who held most of the scientific positions at the time.

Q: The scientists interviewed are all Christians. How do they say science and faith are related?

A: Both science and faith are concerned with the search for truth (John Polkinghorne gave the example of a boiling kettle – see the Briefing Sheet: Beyond Reason?).

Chapter 2

Q: What different views did the scientists in the documentary express on the Big Bang?

A: All the scientists believe that God created the universe – and that, according to the current theory, God created using the Big Bang. Also, science doesn't know yet what happened right at the start of the Big Bang.

Q: Why aren't the gaps in scientific knowledge good proof for God?

A: One reason is because scientists may be able to explain them in the future.

An example of 'God of the gaps' was given here by David Wilkinson, who used to believe that God was needed to light the 'blue touch paper' (the fuse) at the beginning of the Big Bang. But the famous physicist Stephen Hawking has come up with a workable theory for what happened before the Big Bang, so the 'blue touch paper' argument isn't a great one anymore, because one day it may be proved wrong.

(Another reason is given in the Discussion Topic for Chapter 2 below, 'The Big Bang': God is at work in everything, not just the 'gaps'.)

Chapter 3

Q: What is fine-tuning (the Anthropic Principle)?

A: It is the idea that the universe has been finely tuned to allow the existence of life.

Chapter 4

> **Q:** Why are the scientists in the documentary not worried about the multiverse theory?
>
> **A:** The multiverse is a theory with absolutely no evidence behind it. Even if there were evidence, God is still sovereign over all that he made, multiverses included.

> **Q:** Can science answer the question: 'Why is there something, rather than nothing?'
>
> **A:** No. Science cannot answer that type of question. We need science and faith to make sense of the world.

Glossary	
atheist	Someone who believes that no gods exist.
cosmologist	Someone who scientifically studies the origin, development and overall shape and nature of the universe.
fine-tuning (the Anthropic Principle)	The idea that the physical constants of the universe are set at the precise values necessary for the existence of biological life.
God of the gaps	An argument which says that when we can't explain something in nature scientifically, that is proof that God exists.
metaphysic	Any particular way of interpreting the world.
multiverse theory	The idea that there are multiple universes. Some people use this to argue that if there are many universes, it's not so surprising that one of them is 'fine-tuned' for life.

Discussion Topics *(25–30 minutes)*

The topics below relate to each of the four DVD chapters. Pick one or two to discuss. You may want to watch the relevant chapter again as a refresher, especially if you are spreading the course over more than one session.

(?) Chapter 1: How Do People See the World? *Level: Intermediate*

> *The aim is to help people to discuss different ways of relating science and faith, and to think about the difference between scientific evidence and the interpretation of that evidence. (The Discussion Topic for Chapter 4 also deals with this question.)*

Dr Ard Louis said that the debate between science and religion is really about how we decide whether something is true or false: is science the only reliable way of finding things out about the world, or does religion have something valuable to contribute as well? [Time code: 1 min. 28]

> **Q1:** With this in mind, what views have you heard from scientists (either in the media or that you have met personally) on the questions, 'Does God exist?' and 'How does God interact with the universe?'
>
> *Hints:*
> *Discussion here will link back to the introductory activity. The main views you could discuss are:*
>
> ***Answer 'no' to the existence of God:***
> * *Science answers every important question. God doesn't exist (scientism/atheistic materialism).*
>
> ***Answer 'yes' to the existence of God:***
> * *There is a god that started the universe going, but that god doesn't interact with us (deism).*
> * *God created and sustains the universe, shared our human nature by coming to live among us in the person of Jesus Christ and interacts with us day by day (Christianity).*

There's a difference between scientific evidence and the interpretation of that evidence. It is possible for people of any religion or none to come up with the same results when they run the same experiment – but how do you interpret that evidence? Obviously some interpretations will be more reliable than others. The truth of a particular interpretation can be tested with more experiments.

Q2: Which of the views above (scientism/atheistic materialism, deism or Christianity) do you think could fit with the evidence the scientists have described about the universe in the documentary?

Hints:

- *To be an atheist you must either believe in some sort of multiverse – which is also a step of faith – or that the whole thing is an incredible coincidence.*

- *A single finely-tuned universe is compatible with deism, Christianity, and indeed many other religions. Session 1b explores the fact that scientific arguments will not get you all the way to Christianity – they only open the discussion (and in the bonus DVD clips for this session two scientists talk about what other factors are important for their faith).*

(?) Chapter 2: The Big Bang

Level: Easy

In this chapter of the DVD the narrator asks the question, 'Hasn't the Big Bang done away with the need for a Creator?'

Q1: What do you think? Do you think God could have created through the Big Bang?

To help your discussion:

- *You could look at the Briefing Sheet: The Big Bang (in Appendix 2).*

- *You could look at the answer to the first Short Question for Chapter 2 of the DVD.*

- *Try not to get onto the interpretation of Genesis – explain that Session 2 will address this. The question of the age of the universe or the interpretation of Genesis need not be tackled here – in fact, some people believe in both a Big Bang and a young universe. You could explain that while it may be difficult for some to ignore the question of the interpretation of Genesis when thinking about the Big Bang, it's important to introduce what most scientists believe. If the answer to the question for some is simply 'no', that's fine – move on and address that issue in more depth later, in Session 2.*

Note: *Scientists used to think that the universe had no beginning. But when the Big Bang was proposed, some atheists didn't like the new theory because it gave the universe a beginning and suggested a Creator.*

God of the gaps?

" If you say, well, science answers this much about the way the universe is, but science doesn't answer this aspect of the universe's characteristics, and then to invoke God and to **allow God to reside in that gap in our knowledge, that's dangerous** because when a clever scientist comes along that gap will be filled by a deeper and richer scientific understanding. So then, where you posit that God is allowed to reside, gets smaller and smaller and smaller, and this is a practice known as **God of the gaps,** and it's dangerous.

Professor Katherine Blundell [Time code: 13 min. 19]

Read Colossians 1:15–17 and Hebrews 1:3a.

Q2: Where do we see God at work? What do these passages say about this idea of not putting 'God in the gaps'?

Hints:

- *God created, upholds and sustains the whole universe.*

- *We see God at work in everything – whether we understand it scientifically or not.*

Note:

- *David Wilkinson, who used to believe that God was needed to light the 'blue touch paper' (the fuse) at the beginning of the Big Bang, gives an example of 'God of the gaps'. But the famous physicist Stephen Hawking has come up with a workable theory for what happened before the Big Bang, so the 'blue touch paper' argument isn't a great one anymore, because one day it may be proved wrong. [Time code: 11 min. 18]*

- *See the section below for a discussion of whether the Anthropic Principle is a gap.*

SESSION 1

See pages 10-11 of the **Study Guide**

Prayer and Miracles

'God of the gaps' raises the question: 'Do scientists, even if they are Christians, believe that God cannot, or will not, work miracles?' Not at all. Here is why:

" While some biblical miracles, such as … the plague of locusts in Egypt, do not directly contradict the laws of nature, other miracles are obviously supernatural. So does science challenge our belief in miracles? … **Christians believe that God, not natural laws, govern nature.** God typically works through natural laws to sustain the regular patterns of our world, but nature is not locked into those patterns.

> Deborah and Loren Haarsma, *Origins* (Faith Alive Christian Resources, 2007), p. 41.

" **I believe God can choose to step out of his regular pattern and do something different at times,** but it would be for a reason relating to an answer to prayer, or something about God's desire to interact spiritually with his people. So I see miracles of healing, miracles in human history, or miracles in the Bible that God used to establish his chosen people and develop a relationship with them. It seems less likely that God would do miracles in natural history that we couldn't discover until modern science.

> Deborah Haarsma, *Test of Faith: Spiritual Journeys with Scientists,* page 97

Q3: How would you define a 'miracle'?

Hint:

- *A miracle is a sign of God's special grace that involves a particularly significant timing or God working in an unusual way in the world, sometimes but not always in response to specific prayer.*

Q4: How does this match your own experience or knowledge of the Bible?

To help your discussion:

- *Not everyone will have experienced something 'miraculous', but they may have experienced answers to prayer and will probably know about some of the miracles recorded in the Bible.*

But are these scientists filling the gap with science instead of God? Is this 'science of the gaps'?

There are always unanswered questions in science. Christians working in science are aware that there could be a 'supernatural' explanation for something being the way it is, but the early scientists – who believed in a Creator God – believed that they should investigate creation, and they found answers to their questions. Rather than mourning the apparent loss of mystery in creation, they rejoiced that they understood God's creation a little bit more and were able to praise God for creating the details they had just uncovered. Christians who are scientists still follow in that tradition, and it is their job to keep looking for answers to their further questions. The more we find out, the further we realize we have to go.

Q5: How do you think these two concepts, miracles and 'God of the gaps', fit together for a Christian?

Hints:

- *Science has nothing to say about miracles, and Christians who are also scientists believe that they do happen – most importantly, the resurrection.*
- *But God is unlikely to have made something happen in the world in a miraculous way if it has nothing to do with God's relationship with people. When there is a gap in knowledge about the way the world works, a scientific explanation may well be found in the end. So if that gap has been used to say, 'This is evidence that God exists!' and a person's faith has been built on that 'evidence', then if the gap is closed that faith will falter.*

(?) Chapter 3: Fine-tuning

Level: In-depth

Q1: **What do you think of the idea of fine-tuning? Do you think it's reasonable to say that the universe as we know it is finely tuned for life (the Anthropic Principle)?**

This question gives people a chance to say what they think about the idea of fine-tuning and the evidence presented to them.

To help your discussion:

- • *You could look at the Briefing Sheet: The Anthropic Principle.*
- • *Don't worry too much about this question if people feel overwhelmed by the scientific detail. If they understand the principle of fine-tuning, move on and discuss the implications.*

Q2: **Earlier, the documentary warned us not to believe in a 'God of the gaps.' But could the idea of fine-tuning be a gap? Think about the difference between the evidence for fine-tuning and the gaps where people have put God in the past (e.g., as an explanation for changes in the weather).**

Hints:

- • *The Anthropic Principle came out of modern science, when astronomers and physicists began to ask questions of the data they had.*
- • *So fine-tuning doesn't appear to be a gap in knowledge about how the universe came to be, but rather a gap in what questions science can answer. We can see from the data that the universe is finely-tuned. 'Why?' is a different question – science cannot answer that question, and the work of a Creator God seems to be the most reasonable answer. This theistic conclusion has prompted some scientists to propose the multiverse theory as an explanation, although other scientists propose the multiverse for purely mathematical reasons.*

Note: *Some scientists say that even the surprise discovery of evidence for multiple universes, or of a mechanism by which the laws are fine-tuned, would not explain the fine-tuning. If a new theory predicts the finely-tuned constants (laws), or a multiverse, you still have to explain the theory. The 'specialness' is now in the theory rather than in the constants. You just moved the problem, you didn't take it away. (For more on this, see the 'Taking it Further' list.) And an even deeper question is: Why is there something rather than nothing? To express the point in the words of the cosmologist Stephen Hawking: 'Why does the universe go to all the bother of existing?'*

Professor Alister McGrath thinks that fine-tuning is consistent with the idea of a God but that it doesn't prove God's existence. [Time code: 18 min. 16]

Q3: **Even if fine-tuning *were* evidence for the existence of God, why couldn't it completely prove God's existence?**

Hints:

There are three possible answers to the question of fine-tuning:

- a. *It is evidence in favour of the existence of God (but we're not saying it's complete proof for God, because of the reason given in [c] below).*
- b. *There is a multiverse or some other explanation, which moves the problem from the observation of finely-tuned physical constants to the theory that predicts the constants (see the note above for Q2).*
- c. *The alternative that cannot be ruled out is that the world is just the way it is. Whether or not that is satisfying depends on your point of view. This is a real reason why, logically, fine-tuning cannot be an absolute proof for God's existence.*

Q4: If fine-tuning was evidence for the existence of God, what kind of God would it be evidence for?

The aim is to show that this is evidence for a god, but this argument does not get you any further than that.

Hints:

A powerful one! This could be:

1. *A mind or force.*
2. *A god who set up the universe and then turned his back. A god who does not interact with us (deism).*
3. *The God of Christianity who made, sustains and interacts with the universe.*
4. *The gods of other religions.*

(?) Chapter 4: How Do You View Science and Faith? *Level: Intermediate*

The aim here is to help people be aware of some different ways of relating science and faith so that at this stage in the course they can reflect on where they might stand on the question of how science and faith relate to each other. You may want to revisit this at the end of the course (Session 3b gives some 'debrief' Epilogue Options).

Some of the most common ways of relating science and faith are:

1. They're in conflict: they ask the same questions and get different results.	2. They're the same: *either* faith can be explained entirely by science, or science can be explained by faith.	3. They're complementary: science and faith ask different questions, and there are some areas where they can overlap and interact	4. They're non-overlapping: they ask different questions.

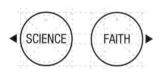

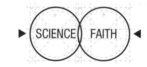

Q: Which do you most agree with, and why?

Hints:

- *None of these are 'right'; they are just different concepts to help people to think about science and faith.*
- *Most of the scientists interviewed in Test of Faith would be closest to the 'complementary' view.*
- *John Polkinghorne's kettle illustration is a good explanation of this complementary view (see the Briefing Sheet: Beyond Reason?).*

If you can think of a different way of relating science and faith, sketch your own diagram below.

Recap

If you used Option 1 as an Introduction, you could go back over the questions and discuss the answers. If the group members are confident, they may be willing to say what they thought before the session and whether they have changed their minds on any of these points.

The message of the documentary (in capitals) was that:

Q1: **Science and faith are at war**
A1: FALSE

Q2: **There are some conflicts between science and faith**
A2: SOMETIMES

Q3: **Most of the first scientists in history were Christians**
A3: TRUE

Q4: **When science can't explain something, that is evidence for God**
A4: NOT NECESSARILY

Q5: **When science *can* explain something, you see evidence for God**
A5: TRUE

Q6: **Science and faith are two different ways of looking at the world**
A6: TRUE, BUT THEY AREN'T MUTUALLY EXCLUSIVE

Q7: **Some questions cannot be answered by science**
A7: TRUE

Q8: **If the universe started with a Big Bang, God lit the blue touch paper (the fuse)**
A8: NOT A VERY GOOD ARGUMENT

Q9: **Some scientists think there are many universes**
A9: TRUE

Q10: **Understanding more about nature will help us to learn more about God**
A10: TRUE

Epilogue: Awe and Wonder *(10–15 minutes)*

One of the messages at the end of this part of the documentary is that studying the world God created is a way to learn more about and bring worship to God.

Read one of the following passages as a starter for a time of prayer and worship: Psalm 8; Psalm 19; or John 1:1–5.

Option 1:

Pray though the passage, praising God for what we see in creation. If you broke up into smaller groups for discussion, you could stay in your small groups to pray.

Option 2:

What things in the created world give you a feeling of awe and wonder? You could brainstorm this as a group onto a flipchart or large piece of paper and pray prayers of thankfulness at the end.

If you have non-believers in your group, the group could discuss the relationship between what the passage says about creation and their own sense of wonder at the universe.

Option 3:

Read the passage and then have a time of silence. You could play a piece of music that invokes a feeling of awe.

Option 4:

Pray though some of the issues that came up in the session, and for the rest of the course.

If you have non-believers in your group you could discuss the issues that challenge you most and talk about what you will do, or could help each other to do, to address them. For example: is there anything on the 'Taking it Further' list that you could read?

Some of the group might want to arrange to read the same book and then come together to discuss it.

Option 5:

If you would like to sing, you could use one of the songs or hymns listed in Appendix 3 on page 113.

Taking it Further

Websites *(general introductions):*

Talks, short papers and links: **www.faraday-institute.org**
Articles, interviews and help for Christians working in or studying science (UK): **www.cis.org.uk**
Articles, interviews and help for Christians working in or studying science (USA): **www.asa3.org**

Articles to download on the topic of the universe:

John Polkinghorne, 'The Anthropic Principle and the Science and Religion Debate':
www.st-edmunds.cam.ac.uk/faraday/resources/Faraday%20Papers/Faraday%20Paper%204%20Polkinghorne_EN.pdf

Rodney Holder, 'Is the Universe Designed?':
www.st-edmunds.cam.ac.uk/faraday/resources/Faraday%20Papers/Faraday%20Paper%2010%20Holder_EN.pdf

Michael Poole, 'God and the Big Bang':
http://cis.thevirtualchurch.co.uk/assets/files/articles/Poole_bang.pdf

Rodney Holder, 'God, the Multiverse, and Everything':
http://cis.thevirtualchurch.co.uk/assets/files/Resources/Articles/Article-Archive/rodney_holder_multiverse.pdf

Books *(general introductions):*

Denis Alexander and Robert S. White, *Beyond Belief: Science, Faith and Ethical Challenges* (Lion, 2004; US: Science, Faith, and Ethics: Grid or Gridlock? [Hendrickson, 2006]). *Beyond Belief* introduces the issues – including ethics, the environment and evolution.

Kirsten Birkett, *Unnatural Enemies* (Matthias Media, 1997). This introduction to the relationship between science and faith is written for people with no Christian background.

Francis Collins, *The Language of God: A Scientist Presents Evidence for Belief* (UK: Simon & Schuster, 2006; USA: Free Press, 2006). This is a very easy introduction and includes much of the former director of the Human Genome Project's personal journey from atheism to Christianity. Covers evolution, ethics and the general relationship between science and faith.

Books on the universe:

David Wilkinson, *God, Time and Stephen Hawking* (Monarch, 2001). This is an easy but thought-provoking introduction to science and theology.

John Polkinghorne, *Quarks, Chaos and Christianity* (UK: SPCK, 2005; USA: Crossroad, 2005). This is John Polkinghorne's most introductory level book. Much of it focuses on physics and astronomy.

SESSION 1

Session 1 Sheet 1:
Negative statements about science and Christianity

Science has disproved God.

Now that we know about evolution it's irrational to believe that God made the world.

I think that everything we do can be explained scientifically.

Religion can all be explained psychologically.

We're just made up of molecules – soon scientists will know how we think, and then we'll know for certain that there's no purpose in life.

Most scientists are atheists.

People used to believe in God because they couldn't explain things like lightning, but now that we know how everything works scientifically we don't need to invent a God to believe in.

So-called 'miracles' can all be explained scientifically; they don't really happen.

There's no evidence for the existence of God – soon no one will believe in him.

Science is about facts and religion is about faith – only superstitious people are religious.

The church tortured Galileo and made him give up science. Christians have always been against science and anything rational.

Session 1 Sheet 2: Quotes about science and Christianity

Atheists

"You clearly can be a scientist and have religious beliefs. But I don't think that you can be a real scientist in the deepest sense of the word because they are such alien categories of knowledge.

Peter Atkins, Professor of Chemistry, Oxford University

"A miracle is a violation of the laws of nature … the proof against a miracle … is as entire as any argument from experience can possibly be imagined.

David Hume, eighteenth-century philosopher

"Galileo, and the astronomers who came after him, dealt a blow to the church from which it can never hope to recover.

Margaret Knight (1903–83), psychologist and humanist, University of Aberdeen

"Unless at least half my colleagues are dunces, there can be – on the most raw and empirical grounds – no conflict between science and religion.

Stephen Jay Gould (1941–2002), Professor of Zoology, Harvard University

"There is no reason to suppose that science cannot deal with every aspect of existence.

Peter Atkins, Professor of Chemistry, Oxford University

"Man at last knows that he is alone in the unfeeling immensity of the universe, out of which he emerged only by chance. Neither his destiny nor his duty have been written down.

Jacques Monod, Nobel Prize-winning molecular biologist and author of *Chance and Necessity*

"Most people, I believe, think that you need a god to explain the existence of the world, and especially the existence of life. They are wrong, but our education system is such that many people don't know it.

Richard Dawkins, former Professor of the Public Understanding of Science, Oxford University

Christians

"Science is dealing with things that are given. Attitudes of awe, wonder and humility before the facts are essential if man is to be in harmony with both his environment and his Creator.

Sir John Houghton, former chair of the scientific panel of the Nobel Prize-winning Intergovernmental Panel on Climate Change

"When we come to the scientifically unknown, our correct policy is not to rejoice because we have found God, it is to become better scientists.

Charles Coulson (1910–74), Professor of Theoretical Chemistry, Oxford University

"Let no man … think or maintain, that a man can search too far, or be too well studied in the Book of God's Word, or in the Book of God's Works – Divinity or Philosophy.

Sir Francis Bacon, one of the founders of modern scientific method

"This most beautiful system of the sun, planets and comets could only proceed from the counsel and dominion of an intelligent being.

Sir Isaac Newton

"… an endemic hostility between science and religion could well be a cultural artefact, reflecting social tensions, aspirations and fears in the nineteenth century.

Colin Russell, Emeritus Professor of History of Science and Technology, the Open University

"Many Philosophers have ruled out metaphysics … Yet this means that there is nowhere left to stand to justify science.

Roger Trigg, Emeritus Professor of Philosophy, Warwick University

"The most important questions in life are not susceptible to solution by the scientific method.

Bill Newsome, Professor of Neurobiology, Stanford University

"The work of a scientist involved in this project, particularly a scientist who has the joy of also being a Christian, is a work of discovery which can also be a form of worship.

Dr Francis Collins, former Director of the Human Genome Project

Bonus Session 1b: Beyond Reason? Facts and Faith

Planning

Aim

This session is more personal and practical than Session 1. It will help the group to explore the interface between science, or a scientific way of thinking, and their own faith.

The DVD clips for this session expand on some of the themes from Part 1 of the documentary and, together with the questions, will explore these themes:

- The questions that science and faith answer
- The fact that faith and evidence are both important in Christian life
- The 'intelligibility' of the universe
- The personal nature of God
- Another look at the Big Bang – beginning with a way to understand the huge distances in the universe
- The multiverse – thinking about evidence and faith

Equipment needed

- You will need to use the DVD bonus interviews for this session. See the 'bonus features' section of the DVD for details.
- If using Introduction Option 1, photocopy and cut out the quotes on Sheet 1 (page 37). If you have a large group, bring Blu-Tack and coloured stickers as well.

Some suggestions for a 1 ½ – 2 hour session:

	Basic introduction	In-depth	Big picture	A group with a lot of scientific knowledge
Introduction Option	1	2	2	2
Ch. 1: Facts and Faith	✓		✓	
Ch. 2: Intelligibility		✓	✓	✓
Ch. 3: A Personal God		✓	✓	✓
Ch. 4: The Big Bang	✓			
Ch. 5: The Multiverse		✓		✓
Epilogue Option	any	any	any	any

To split into two shorter sessions *(40–60 minutes each)*

Ask the group to read the material related to this session in the *Study Guide* beforehand.

First half-session:

- Introduction activity in pairs *(5–10 minutes)*
- Discussion Topics – pick one or two
- Epilogue *(5–10 minutes)*

Second half-session:

- Quick recap by leader *(5 minutes)*
- Discussion Topics – pick one or two more
- Epilogue *(5–10 minutes)*

Preparation for Participants *(optional)*:
Why bother thinking about science and faith?

It would be worth doing the preparation for Session 1, if you did not use it already, or:

As a recap of some of the issues covered in the last session, and as an introduction to this session, read one of the articles recommended on the 'Taking it Further' list for Session 1 ('God and the Big Bang' is the most introductory of these).

Introduction *(10–15 minutes)*

Option 1:

Q: What questions does science answer?

Print and cut up Sheet 1 (page 37). Discuss and sort them into three groups:

1. Questions that can be answered by scientific methods
2. Those that can't
3. Questions that can be answered by both scientific and other methods

> *Hints:*
> - *Scientific questions study the natural world by making predictions that are testable by experiment or observation and often use mathematical analysis.*
> - *Not science: 'metaphysical', or impossible to test by experiment. Philosophical or abstract questions.*

> *For larger groups:*
> - *Get people to vote on each question.*
> - *Or ask if someone can suggest an answer and see if others agree.*
> - *You could enlarge each question, fix them around the walls with Blu-Tack and get people to vote by sticking a coloured sticker on the question – e.g., red (science), blue (not science), green (both).*
> - *For a more active group you could designate three corners of the room – science, not science and both, and get people to move to the appropriate corner as you read out the questions.*

Option 2:

Q: Can you think of questions that: A) Science can answer? B) Science cannot answer? C) Both science and faith can answer?

> *Use the hints above to decide what could be answered by science. If you don't have much scientific knowledge between you it may involve a fair bit of speculation, but it should be a good way to get people to think about what science is.*

Discussion Topics *(60–90 minutes)*

Pick two or three of these to discuss. The video clips are on the 'bonus' menu of the DVD.

(?) Facts and Faith   *Level: Easy*

What would you say to someone who said, 'Surely science is about rationality and faith is about irrationality'?

> *The DVD clips reply to this question, and the questions below give people the chance to apply that idea to their own lives, thinking about the difference between faith and rationality and how those two things apply in the decisions they make.*

Watch the bonus interview: 1.1 Ard Louis and John Polkinghorne *(3 min.)*

Glossary	
fideistic	Something that is based solely on faith or revelation, ignoring reason or intellect.

Q1: Can you think of a decision in your life that had an almost entirely rational or logical basis?

Examples:
- *I don't drink tea any more because I'm allergic to caffeine and it will make me sick.*
- *I don't have a dog because I don't like dogs.*
- *I didn't buy a new car because I need to spend my money on something else.*

Q2: Can you think of a decision that involved faith, or trust?

Examples:
- *Getting married, hiring a new person at work, trusting objects (car, chair, parachute!)*

Read Luke 1:1–4 and 1 Corinthians 15:1–11.

Q3: As Ard Louis and John Polkinghorne say in the DVD, logic and faith often overlap. Can you talk about one significant step or decision in your own life and how rationality or faith influenced that decision?

To help your discussion:
- *You might want to ask two or three people in advance if they'd be willing to tell their stories, or break into pairs or smaller groups.*
- *It might be useful to point out that obviously everyone is a work in progress and will not have everything sewn up. Some of the discussions about 'God of the gaps' might have changed a few things for people – and the language of 'proof' may have changed to language of 'evidence', but that's no reason for people's faith to be destabilized.*

? Intelligibility

Level: Easy

The aim of this section is to help people to understand the concept of intelligibility in relation to God as Creator – and then to look at this side by side with the revelation of a personal God.

 Watch the bonus interview: 1.2 Ard Louis *(1 min.)*

Ard Louis refers to the 'deep logos or logic behind the universe'.

Read John 1: 1–3. The 'word' in John 1 is a translation of the Greek word *logos,* from which we get the English word 'logic'. It's generally agreed that John took the Greek idea of *logos*, a mind or rational principle governing the universe, and said that *logos* is Jesus, who was there in the beginning and came to earth as man.

Q1: What do you think of the idea that we can do mathematics because a rational God created the world?

To help your discussion:
- *You could also watch the section in the DVD again where Ard Louis talks about Dirac and antimatter (2 min.) [Time code: 8 min. 53 to 10 min. 54]*

A Personal God

Read John 1: 4–5.

 Watch the bonus interview: 1.3 John Polkinghorne and Katherine Blundell *(3 min.)*

> **Q2:** **All of the scientists interviewed have an experience of a personal God. What evidence or experiences show this personal God: A) for Christians in general; and B) for you?**
>
> *Part A) should be easy to answer, and B) will give people a chance to think through the non-scientific evidence that helps them to have faith. You could break into smaller groups for this question.*

 # The Big Bang   *Level: Intermediate*

This is a mainly scientific section for those who have not studied much astronomy or physics in the past, or who need a refresher.

You could also use the Briefing Sheet: The Big Bang to provide more background for your discussion.

 Watch the bonus interview: 1.4 Deborah Haarsma *(30 sec.)*

> **Q1:** **A light year is the distance light travels in a year (about 6 trillion miles). Imagine light leaving the earth when you were born. What was happening in the world then? If you imagine TV pictures of those things being beamed out across the universe, where will they have reached now?**

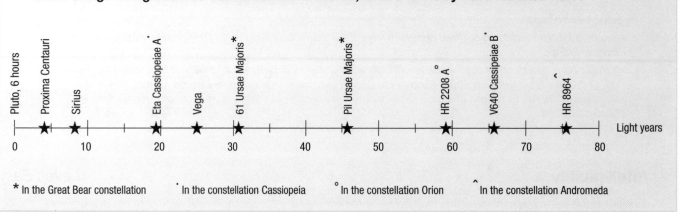

You can think about this the other way around, too. If you use a telescope to look at the night sky, some of the light that you can see began its journey when you were born. Around which star is that light coming from?

 Watch the bonus interview: 1.5 David Wilkinson *(3 min. 30 sec.)*

Glossary	
cosmology	The study of the origin, development and overall shape and nature of the universe.
order of magnitude	Most commonly used to mean ten times larger (e.g., 5,000 is two orders of magnitude larger than 50).

How have Christians responded to Big Bang theory? Here are three views that Christians hold:

A. God made the universe and everything in it supernaturally about 10,000 years ago, as described in Genesis 1. The scientific evidence for the Big Bang and the great age of the universe is faulty. Creation scientists have suggested other possible explanations for the vast scale of the universe and the distance light must travel.

B. God made the universe and everything in it supernaturally about 10,000 years ago, as described in Genesis 1. Scientists are correct about the evidence for the age of the universe, but this is only an appearance of history. Everything was created with this history built in: trees with rings representing hundreds of years, light already on the way from stars billions of light years away, etc.

C. The scientific evidence for the Big Bang is correct. God used the Big Bang to make the universe 13.7 billion years ago and has been sustaining it ever since. Christians holding this view have different ways of reconciling this with Genesis 1, which will be discussed in Session 2.

Q2: Which of these views have you come across before?

To help your discussion:

- *Session 2 will deal with the interpretation of Genesis, so this will begin the discussion and may just raise some issues that can be left for further discussion in future weeks.*

Note: *If you look at the Briefing Sheet: Views on Genesis 1, A and B match view 1, and C matches views 2 and 3.*

SESSION 1

(?) The Multiverse   *Level: Intermediate*

The aim of this section is to spend a bit more time thinking about idea of a multiverse and how Christian scientists respond to it – and then to think further about faith and evidence from science.

 Watch the bonus interview: 1.6 Deborah Haarsma and David Wilkinson *(2 min.)*

Glossary

Particle physics   The study of the tiny particles that make up atoms.

Q1: What are some of the different scientific responses to the idea of the multiverse that the documentary gives?

Hints:

- *John Polkinghorne doesn't think other universes are there.*
- *David Wilkinson thinks they might be there.*
- *Katherine Blundell advises to proceed with caution – this is not something we can test scientifically.*
- *Peter Harrison says this is more like a religious question, not something we can test scientifically.*

To help your discussion:

- *You may want to watch the section in the DVD again that refers to the multiverse idea (4 min. 15 – Time code: 18 min. 54 to 23 min. 09).*

Q2: Several of the interviewees mention how they feel about the idea of the multiverse as Christians. What are their views? Based on your knowledge of the Bible, do you think there are any arguments for or against the idea of the multiverse?

Hints:

- *Jennifer Wiseman, John Polkinghorne and David Wilkinson say the multiverse is not a problem theologically because we have a big, generous God who is free to create as he likes.*
- *You could look at Isaiah 55:8–9 (a big God who can do what he likes) and Matthew 14:13–21 (a generous God).*

See page 19 of the **Study Guide**

 Watch the bonus interview: 1.7 David Wilkinson *(1 min. 30 sec.)*

Q3: What is the difference between evidence and proof? Can you think of any examples?

Evidence: You come across a spot in the road with tyre marks, broken glass and a twisted bumper lying in the verge, but no sign of smashed up cars. Nonetheless, the evidence does seem to point to the fact that a car accident happened there recently.

Proof: A situation where the conclusions follow inevitably from the starting point, which is why the word is used more in maths than in the experimental sciences, and hardly at all in biology.

Q4: Keeping all this in mind, what do you think is the most helpful way to look at evidence in science and relate that to faith?

Hints:

- *There is evidence in science that is consistent with our faith (e.g., the Anthropic Principle).*
- *But we cannot rely on this evidence as absolute proof because new theories do emerge.*
- *We look at any of this evidence alongside the evidence based on our own experiences of God, the Bible, other historical evidence for the Christian faith, etc. A faith based on science alone would certainly be shaky, but when faith is based on experience of God - revealed through history, through Jesus and the experience of Christian life now – we can see that faith is consistent with the findings of science.*
- *Also, looking at what God has revealed through nature can sometimes get people thinking about whether there is a God or not, and it can help them to realize that it is quite reasonable to believe in a Creator God. But they need to go further, and find out about God in other ways, or they will remain 'deists'.*

Epilogue: Supporting Christians in Science *(10–15 minutes)*

Option 1:

 Watch the bonus interview: 1.8 David Wilkinson *(1 min.)*

Pray for any people in your church who are involved in scientific studies, research or teaching.

Option 2:

Use Psalm 8; Psalm 19; or John 1:1–5 as a starter for a time of prayer and reflection. (You could use one of the ideas from the Epilogue for Session 1.)

Option 3:

If you would like to sing, you could use one of the songs or hymns listed in Appendix 3 on page 113.

Taking it Further

See list for Session 1.

Session 1b Sheet 1: Science and Faith, Introductory Questions

Science:

How far is Jupiter from earth?

What is the diameter of a circle with a radius of 10 cm.?

How much chlorine is in my tap water?

Why is the sky blue?

Why is the grass green?

How do mosquitoes reproduce?

Not science:

May I eat that fruit?

Should we try to clone humans?

Why can we explain the universe mathematically?

Why do you love me?

What should I call my child?

Both:

Is a human infant worth more than a fully-grown chimpanzee?

What makes children bully each other?

Why is the kettle boiling?

Why am I here?

Why do I like that picture?

How do you feel?

Test of Faith – Session 1: Beyond Reason? Science, Faith and the Universe
www.testoffaith.com

37

Session 2: An Accident in the Making?
Creation, Evolution and Interpreting Genesis

Introduction to Session 2

Genesis addresses questions that we all ask: 'Why are we here?' 'What are we here for?' 'What makes us special?' There has been much debate about how to interpret Genesis, and there are important questions here for everyone to consider about the origin of human life, the presence of suffering and evil in the world.

Part 2 of the documentary looks briefly at several views on creation before moving on to examine critically the way that some Christians reconcile evolution with the Bible. It then moves beyond the debate to consider one live issue that all Christians have been called to tackle: caring for creation.

Part 2 of the documentary should leave the viewer with the main messages that:

- Christians hold different views on the way God created the world.
- Many believing scientists think that God used evolution to create the world.
- But evolution raises a number of issues for Christians, the main one being suffering.
- Despite our different views on creation, Christians know that God has called them to care for creation – although the healing must first start with the human heart.

Note: The aim of the documentary is to show what the majority of Christians working in science believe, and to examine those beliefs in detail. We felt that it was important to mention other views, but we have not covered these in equal depth because they have already been well communicated and debated in print, film and online. Instead, the documentary examines very closely the implications of 'Theistic Evolution'. (See the 'Taking it Further' list for web links and book recommendations. There are also Briefing Sheets on some of the less well-known topics. You may be able to anticipate which issues will be most likely to interest your group, in which case you could have a few copies of a relevant article printed out for people to take away. If a particular topic sparks interest one week, you could bring extra reading on that topic the following week.)

The fact that God created the universe is one of the vital messages of Christianity. God is capable of acting in any way he chooses. God is intimately involved with his creation – not only by sustaining everything, but also by making direct and personal contact with the people within it, including 'supernatural' miracles when he chooses (see Session 1). The resurrection is the most important of these miracles. While all Christians are united in their belief in God as Creator, believing in any particular mechanism of creation is not a benchmark of orthodox Christianity and none of the great church creeds specify this. As such, it is an important subject, open to careful, informed debate, and one about which Christians can hold different views without threatening their unity. The course will equip you to discuss a range of views on creation and come to your own conclusions.

This is not a detailed Bible study on Genesis. Its aim, rather, is to help people to digest the information that the documentary presents and to explore the biblical material underlying the points that it raises. For a more detailed study of Genesis, there are a large number of study guides and commentaries available.

Planning

There are four sessions to help you navigate your way through this topic.* The aim is to introduce the subject to people who are new to it, but you can start at any level depending on where you think the majority of people in your group are. If in doubt, it's probably best to start at the beginning with Session 2 or 2.1.

Session 2: Overview
For those who only have time for one session and want to discuss the DVD more generally.

In-depth Session 2.1: Interpreting Genesis
Different views on the interpretation of Genesis

In-depth Session 2.2: An Accident in the Making?
Some questions about the process and timescale of evolution

In-depth Session 2.3: Evolution, Suffering and the Fall
Some more difficult questions concerning human evolution, the fall and suffering

*In-depth Sessions 2.1–2.3 do not cover the environment, so you should use either the environment section from Session 2: Overview or Bonus Session 2b: The Environment.

Test of Faith – Session 2: An Accident in the Making? Creation, Evolution and Interpreting Genesis 39
www.testoffaith.com

SESSION 2

Session 2: Overview

Planning

Aim

This session gives an overview of the topics that the DVD covers. You may wish to dip into the in-depth sessions (2.1, 2.2 or 2.3) if any topics give rise to a lot of discussion.

Equipment needed

- If you will be using Epilogue Option 2, you will need blank paper and pens.

Some suggestions for a 1 ½ – 2 hour session:

	Basic introduction	In-depth	Big picture	A group with a lot of scientific knowledge
Introduction Option	2	4	3	1
DVD	✓	✓	✓	✓
Ch. 1: Views on Creation	✓	✓		✓
Ch. 2: Human Evolution				✓
Ch. 3: A Random Process?			✓	
Ch. 4: Suffering		✓		
Ch. 5: Caring for Creation	✓		✓	
Epilogue Option	1	4	5	3

To split into two shorter sessions *(40–60 minutes each)*

Ask the group to read the material related to this session in the *Study Guide* beforehand.

First half-session:

- Introduction activity in pairs *(5 minutes)*
- DVD – watch and discuss for 5 minutes after each chapter
- Epilogue *(5 minutes)*

Second half-session:

- Quick recap by leader *(5 minutes)*
- Finish watching DVD if needed
- Discussion Topics – pick one or two that raised the most interest, or split into smaller groups to discuss different topics
- Epilogue *(5 minutes)*

Preparation for Participants *(optional)*:
Views on creation

If you had to explain your own views on creation, what would you say?

or

Ask two or three friends, family members or colleagues what they think about how the universe, with our planet and all the life we see on it, came to be.

If you use this activity, Introduction Option 1 would be the most appropriate to use.

Introduction *(10–15 minutes)*

This section should help people to see the relevance of talking about creation in detail –because people do hold different views and because it raises some big questions about life and how we got to be here.

Option 1:

Q: Christians agree that God created the earth, but they hold different views about how the creation accounts in Genesis relate to scientific discoveries. What different views are you aware of?

To help your discussion:
- *You could use the Briefing Sheet: Views on Genesis 1 if people need a refresher on these.*
- *You might want to go back to the question, 'How do you view science and faith?' from Session 1.*
- *You could return to these views at the end of the session, if you use Epilogue Option 2.*

Option 2:

Q: What recent experiences have made you stop and think about the incredible variety of living things in the world?

Option 3:

Q: Five-year-olds are great at asking unanswerable questions. What are the most difficult questions you've heard someone ask?

Hint:
- *Probably people will come up with questions about suffering, as well as questions about where life and human beings came from. These are important questions and, while this session clearly can't answer them all for you, it will help you to begin to look at a few of the underlying issues.*

Option 4:

Q: Why did God create the world? How did he feel about it then? And now?

Hint:
- *This is a bit of a theoretical question! The idea is to get people thinking about God's act of creation and what it means for the world to be a creation.*
- *You could use Genesis 1:31 as a help for 'How did he feel about it then?'*

SESSION 2

Watch *Test of Faith* Part 2: An Accident in the Making?
(45–60 minutes)

This part of the documentary covers several different views on creation. You might want to mention this and ask people to be ready to evaluate the different arguments presented for each position.

Use the chapter menu to watch Part 2 of the documentary a chapter at a time. Pause the DVD at the end of each chapter using the cues below (press pause after you hear the cue).

Chapter 1 – Narrator: 'For Young Earth Creationism and Intelligent Design, then, Darwinian evolution is an enemy to faith.' [Time code: 10 min. 05]

Chapter 2 – Narrator: 'This marriage of Darwin's theory and faith is known as Theistic Evolution.' [Time code: 14 min. 33]

Chapter 3 – Simon Conway Morris: '… are they themselves in any way congruent with those world pictures?' [Time code: 18 min. 27]

Chapter 4 – Alister McGrath: '… and until science confronts that enigma, we're stuck.' [Time code: 26 min. 00]

Chapter 5 – Denis Alexander: '… to be good stewards of the earth, to care for the earth in the right kind of way.' [Time code: 29 min. 03]

*But if your group members are quite familiar with Young Earth Creationism and Intelligent Design, we suggest you watch through to the end of Chapter 2, without pausing for discussion.

Note: The last chapter of Part 2 is the trailer for Part 3, so you could play it at the end of the session to inspire people to come again.

After each chapter take a few minutes (depending on the size of your group) to help people process what they have just seen. For general discussion use an open question such as:

- What was new or most interesting for you?
- What did you find most surprising or challenging?
- What do you think the main messages were?
- What do you think? Do you agree?

Or you could use the Short Questions below.

Short Questions:

Chapter 1

Q: What are the two different views on creation we've heard so far? (The next chapter will explain a third view.)

A1:   There is *no* good evidence for an earth hundreds of millions of years old. If you want to take the Bible seriously you should believe what it says about the earth being created in six days.

A2:   That there are signs of intentional design in creation.

Chapter 2

Q: What is the third view on creation?

A: That evolution can fit within a Christian framework. This is called 'Theistic Evolution' or 'Evolutionary Creationism'.

Q: What's a metaphysical framework? What does that have to do with a scientific concept like evolution?

A: A metaphysical framework is a set of ideas through which we understand how the world works. Everyone works within a metaphysical framework of guiding ideas in life – and that can include religious and philosophical views, such as Christianity or atheism, that are impossible to test by experiment. Simon Conway Morris thinks that evolutionary biology is compatible with several metaphysical frameworks, but that the one that makes the best sense is Christianity.

Session 1 (in the Discussion Topic 'How do people see the world?') and Session 1b (in the Introduction Option 1: 'What questions does science answer?') cover these ideas.

Chapter 3

Q: **What are the two meanings of the word 'random' that Ard Louis describes?**

A1: In day-to-day life we use it to mean 'purposeless'.

A2: In a scientific sense it means that the microscopic details of a process may be unpredictable, but the overall process may be very predictable.

Q: **Which meaning does he says fits with evolution?**

A: The second.

Chapter 4

Q: **The biggest challenge to faith that comes from evolution is the role of suffering and death in the process. How do the two scientists here, John Polkinghorne and Francis Collins, answer that challenge?**

A: Both agree that it's a difficult question and does not have a completely satisfactory answer.

John Polkinghorne thinks that it is a more positive thing for a loving God to make a creation that can 'make itself', than for God to simply make it (and us) with no freedom, and therefore no opportunity for evil. Such evil may be 'an inescapable shadow side' that comes from creation being able to produce life.

Francis Collins thinks that this may be the only way to make a good and stable universe for us to live in.

Q: **What is the source of hope that Alister McGrath gives us in the first comment?**

A: The New Testament tells us that competition was not the ultimate plan for our lives – the physically strong will not triumph over the weak.

Chapter 5

Q: **What two reasons does the DVD give for why Christians should care for the environment?**

A1: God commands us to care for creation in Genesis.

A2: Caring for the environment is an important way of caring for the poor.

Glossary	
DNA	The chemical molecule inside every cell of every living thing that carries the instructions for its growth and development.
Intelligent Design	The idea that some parts of living things are too complex to have evolved, coupled with the idea that the information contained in DNA cannot have arisen by a process describable in purely material terms, so providing evidence for 'design'.
Theistic Evolution (or Evolutionary Creationism)	The belief that God created life through the process of evolution.
Young Earth Creationism	The belief that Genesis should be interpreted as a literal, historical and scientific account, and therefore that God created the world between 6,000 and 10,000 years ago in six twenty-four hour days.

Discussion Topics *(25–30 minutes)*

The topics below relate to each of the five DVD chapters. Pick one or two to discuss. You may want to watch the relevant chapter again as a refresher, especially if you are spreading the course over more than one session.

> **Note:** *If you are going to use Session 2b: The Environment, you should miss out Chapter 5, below.*

SESSION 2

(?) Chapter 1: Views on Creation

Level: Easy

Read Genesis 1.

Q1: What are the most important messages of this passage? What does it say about God? About God's relationship with the universe? About God's relationship with people?

Hints:

- *There is one God.*
- *God existed before creation.*
- *He is the 'first cause' of creation: the reason creation exists.*
- *He actively created the world.*
- *He is independent of creation and has complete power over it.*
- *He cares about creation.*
- *What God created is good.*
- *God made us in his image.*
- *God cares about us.*
- *We care for creation at God's command.*

Q2: What do you think of the different views on creation that the documentary presented? Were any of them new to you?

This is a subject that some people may have thought and read about in some detail. The aim is to let people (briefly) air their views, perhaps before moving on to a more detailed discussion using one of the following Discussion Topics.

To help your discussion:
The three views are:

1. *There is no good evidence for an earth hundreds of millions of years old. If you want to take the Bible seriously you should believe what it says about the earth being created in six days.*
2. *That there are signs of intentional design in creation.*
3. *That evolution can fit within a Christian framework. This is called 'Theistic Evolution', or 'Evolutionary Creationism'.*

You could also use the Briefing Sheet: Views on Genesis 1. Intelligent Design theory makes no claim to be a religious view, but it is compatible with certain forms of all three of the views outlined on the Briefing Sheet: Views on Genesis 1.

Q3: Thinking back to the main messages you picked out in Genesis 1, how would you say the views on creation that you just discussed in Q2 complement or contradict the biblical material?

Hint:

- *You will probably hear some interesting insights but no real contradictions to the main messages people picked out. We return to the idea that this is a secondary issue, so it's possible for Christians to hold different views.*

(?) Chapter 2: Human Evolution

Level: In-depth

Read Genesis 2:4–25 and the Briefing Sheet: Views on Genesis 2 and 3, Who were Adam and Eve?

Q1: Which of these views do you think could fit best with the biblical and scientific account?

To help your discussion:
You could also use the Briefing Sheet: Views on Genesis 1 to find where these views come from in terms of interpreting Genesis 1. Which of the views on Adam and Eve could be compatible with each view on Genesis 1?

So how are we special compared to other animals? The Bible says that we are made 'in God's image'. We'll explore the implications of this further in Bonus Session 3b, but for now we're interested in how that came to be.
There are several ways to see this:

1. We were specially created as we are – evolution had no part to play.

2. God took evolved *Homo sapiens* and breathed immortal souls into them.

3. There was a growing spiritual awareness in *Homo sapiens*.

For all three views, there is a point of coming into relationship with God. The image of God is something God gives to each one of us and has nothing to do with our own abilities.

It would be impossible to know the details for any of these possibilities but, whatever happened, at least as far as positions 2 and 3 are concerned, at some point a pair or group of creatures came into personal relationship with God.

Q2: Which of the three 'image of God' views, above, fit to which 'Who were Adam and Eve?' views on the Briefing Sheet? What do you think of these views, and how they fit the biblical account?

Hints:
- *View 1 fits A, B*
- *View 2 fits C, D and E*
- *View 3 fits C, D and E*

(?) Chapter 3: A Random Process?   Level: Easy

The aim of this section is to examine the role of randomness in evolution. In-depth Session 2.2 will look at 'convergence'.

Dr Ard Louis said that the word 'random' can mean two things:

- In everyday life we use it to mean 'purposeless'.
- From a scientific way of thinking it means that the tiny details are unpredictable – while the overall process can still be very predictable.

And it's clear that evolution is the scientific type of random process: it acts as a 'random optimizer' to find the best solution to a problem.

[Time code: 15 min. 04]

Read Proverbs 16:33 and Genesis 50:20.

Q1: Keeping in mind the second definition of the word 'random', can you think of something in your life that seemed chaotic or random to you at the time but made sense afterwards?

Q2: What do you think of the idea that God might work in creation in a similar way?

In answering Q1 people may have already mentioned some events that involved God interacting with (the non-human part of) creation. If God is interacting with creation in this way, then could he have been working in the same way in creation before we were on the scene?

Q3: Is it possible that God could be in control of a process like evolution?

The answer may be 'yes, but ...' and people will almost certainly have more questions. The main question we are dealing with here is whether God could potentially work through a seemingly random process like evolution.

(?) Chapter 4: Suffering

Level: In-depth

This section deals with the question of 'physical evil'. Evil caused by human sinfulness is obviously a result of the fall, but what about other sorts of evil? Science is telling us that death, natural disasters and disease have been present in the world since the beginning. How are Christians who accept evolution able to reconcile this with the biblical account?

" The consequences of the evolutionary process are, admittedly, at times things that cause suffering for individuals even today. A child with cancer may well be seen as one of those side-effects of the fact that DNA copying is not perfect, **it's important that DNA copying not be perfect or evolution wouldn't be possible, but if it results in a cancer arising in a child, isn't that a terrible price to pay**? These are difficult questions to be sure. [Time code: 21 min. 03]

Dr Francis Collins

" **Why would a loving God allow a tsunami that would kill hundreds of thousands of people?** There are various explanations; I'm not sure that any of them are completely satisfactory. This is one of the toughest questions that believers have to face. [Time code: 25 min. 03]

Dr Francis Collins

" There is a great danger in tackling this kind of topic that the discussion might seem demeaning to someone personally going through a period of suffering … these are not the kinds of reflections that are likely to be of much help to someone actually passing through a period of suffering (although they might be), but I think they do have pastoral significance in preparing us for times when we will experience suffering in the future.

Dr Denis Alexander, *Creation or Evolution: Do We Have to Choose?* (p. 277)

Read Genesis 3:1–24.

Q1: How would you define 'physical evil'? How is it different from any other kind of evil?

Hints:

- *We call things that happen to us that cause us to experience pain and suffering, and are not caused by human sinfulness, 'physical evil'.*
- *There is a fuzzy line between what we're calling 'physical evil' and the evil that human sinfulness causes. How can you tell whether any particular experience of pain and suffering is caused by human sinfulness or not? We come to this in Q3.*

Q2: What are the possible explanations for the existence of 'physical evil'?

Hint:

- *There are only two real possibilities: either it was always there in creation, or it happened as a consequence of the fall.*

How could pain and suffering be part of God's original plan for us in a world he declared to be 'good'? There are several possible ways of looking at this:

1. Would physical suffering have been experienced as evil before the fall?
2. Would people have been protected from physical suffering in the Garden of Eden?
3. What if the good world was not meant to be a paradise, but the place where people are made ready for eternal life in the new creation?

Q3: What do you think? Do you think that Adam and Eve, even if they didn't die, would have experienced pain and suffering?

To help your discussion:

- *Death is not discussed here – it is a separate issue and dealt with in In-depth Session 2.3: Evolution, Suffering and the Fall.*

Note: We suggest you use Epilogue Option 3 if you use this section.

(?) Chapter 5: Caring for Creation   *Level: Intermediate*

Caring for the environment is not an alternative to the gospel but part of our God-given responsibility to care for the world. It's a responsibility that the whole church needs to take seriously, not just a few 'extra motivated' Christians, and there are many ways we can get involved.

Read Psalm 104.

Q1: What does this psalm tell us about the relationship between God, people and creation?

Hint:

- *God is the Creator and sustainer of everything. We are part of creation and depend on God, just as every other living thing also depends on God.*

Q2: What have you heard recently about environmental issues?

To help your discussion:

- *The purpose of this question is to draw out what people already know and get them thinking broadly about environmental issues.*
- *Try not to focus just on global warming – draw out other issues as well – but you could use the two climate change Briefing Sheets for Session 2 if there is a lot of confusion on that issue.*

Read Genesis 1:26–30 and Genesis 2:15.

Q3: What is the status of people in relation to the rest of creation? What did God command them to do?

Hints:

- *We are the only ones who are made in God's image (Gen. 1:27). (Bonus Session 3b will discuss this further.)*
- *God gives us the same things to eat as the other animals, so we have no special rights to consumption (Gen 1:30). (If the group are tempted to get sidetracked, note that we are not commanded to be vegetarians, see Gen. 9:3.)*
- *God gives us dominion, which means we are given responsibility to care for creation, not to exploit it or have rights over it (Gen. 1:28).*
- *God tells Adam to tend and care for the garden (Gen. 2:15). The Hebrew words here can be translated 'to serve and preserve'.*
- *God released and blessed people to go into the world (Gen. 1:28, like a benediction at the end of a church service). NB: God also blessed and released the sea creatures (Gen. 1:22).*

Q4: What are some ways you can start to care for the environment where you live?

There are a variety of ways, and every little bit we do will help. Look at the 'Activities', 'Taking it Further' and 'personal lifestyle audit' sheets in Bonus Session 2b for ideas (pages 77-80).

Read Colossians 1:15–20 and Romans 8:19–22.

Q5: How can Christians have hope now and hope for the future?

Hints:

- *Now: Colossians 1:15–20 says that Jesus has reconciled all things through his life, death and resurrection. The relationships between human beings and God that were broken in the fall have been restored – but, as we know, this restoration is a work in progress.*
- *Future: Romans 8:19–23 says that this restoration will be completed when we receive our resurrection bodies and live in the 'new heaven and new earth'. Revelation 21 and 22 describe the new creation in figurative language.*

SESSION 2

Epilogue *(10–15 minutes)*

Option 1: Caring for creation

Read Genesis 1:26–28 and Genesis 2:15.

Use the passages above to start a prayer time focusing on our role as stewards of God's creation, and the part scientists have to play in this.

Option 2:

Hand out blank paper and pens for people to make notes of:

1. Anything new they have learned
2. Any conclusions they have come to
3. Any questions they still have
4. Things they'll do to find answers (don't forget the 'Taking it Further' section, with suggested resources).

You could schedule a session where you come back together to talk about what you've found out, and whether your answers to 1–3 have changed. Pray together for inspiration and clarity.

Option 3: A response to the question of suffering

What, ultimately, is God's response to the question of suffering? Two answers are given. Read the passages and use them as the basis for a time of discussion, quiet reflection or prayer.

Job 38:1–7 and Isaiah 55:9

God is in control, and suffering is something we cannot fully understand for the moment. Perhaps we cannot answer the question of suffering on human terms, or judge God by our standards. As the book of Job makes clear, who are we to try to hold God to account? Whatever the answer is, it will be ultimately consistent with God's character as revealed in Scripture.

John 11:32–36; Luke 23:33–43; and Revelation 21:3–5

The gospel. God came to us in the person of Jesus Christ and shared in our suffering. On the cross God was at the mercy of the worst humanity could offer, in addition to experiencing the worst that humanity deserves. In the resurrection Jesus triumphed over death and instigated a new creation which, when it comes to full fruition, will be a place where pain and suffering are abolished. This is the hope we have in the present situation. The Bible's final words on suffering are about the new creation.

Option 4: A higher ethic

We are not called to take our ethics from the animals, with their interactions that are a complex mixture of competition and care, but from the Bible.

" One of the points I'd like to make here is this. As I read the New Testament, I see a whole series of value statements that are completely opposed to Darwinism. It is not the strong who will triumph, it's actually the weak, and so on. And the key point here is that maybe **the gospel actually is saying to us that we need to articulate a system of values which contradict those that we see in nature around us**, that the way nature behave is not the way things are meant to be, that just because species are in competition we don't need to be in competition with each other. It's about a higher ethic than that.

Professor Alister McGrath [Time code 22 min. 27]

Read Philippians 2:1–11 and use it as a starter for a time of quiet reflection and prayer.

Option 5:

If you would like to sing, you could use one of the songs or hymns on the list in Appendix 3 on page 113.

See page 69 for the 'Taking it Further' list.

In-depth Session 2.1: Interpreting Genesis

Planning

Aim

The aim of this session is to look at the different ways of interpreting Genesis, bearing in mind the rationale outlined in the 'Introduction to Session 2' (page 38). The Discussion Topics for Session 2.1 are a sandwich, beginning and ending with consideration of the most important messages in Genesis 1 that are the primary issues for Christians. In between there is an opportunity to look at different views on the interpretation of Genesis, with two optional sections exploring these views in more detail.

It's been our experience that the constituency of most groups will represent a broad range of views, so it is worth covering this session in a reasonable amount of detail without assuming previous knowledge of any particular views.

Equipment needed

- If you are using Epilogue Option 2 you will need to have a world map handy.
- If using Epilogue Option 3, you will need blank paper and pens.

Some suggestions for a 1 ½ – 2 hour session:

	Basic introduction	In-depth	Big picture	A group with a lot of scientific knowledge
Introduction Option	1 or 2	1 or 2	1 or 2	1 or 2
DVD	✓	✓	✓	✓
Genesis 1	✓	✓	✓	✓
Interpreting Genesis	✓	✓	✓	✓
A Deeper Meaning				
A Question of Days		Pick one or use both, as you have time		
What's the Bottom Line?	✓	✓	✓	✓
Epilogue Option	any	any	any	1

To split into two shorter sessions *(40–60 minutes each)*

Ask the group to read the material related to this session in the *Study Guide* beforehand.

First half-session:

- Introduction activity in pairs *(5–10 minutes)*
- DVD – watch *(15 minutes)* and discuss for 5–10 minutes after each chapter
- Epilogue *(5–10 minutes)*

Second half-session:

- Quick recap by leader *(5 minutes)*
- Discussion Topics – use the three basic options *('Genesis 1', 'Interpreting Genesis' and 'What's the Bottom Line?')*
- Epilogue *(5–10 minutes)*

Preparation for Participants *(optional)*:
Views on creation

If you had to explain your own views on creation, what would you say?

or

Ask two or three friends, family members or colleagues what they think about how the universe, with our planet and all the life we see on it, came to be.

Introduction *(10–15 minutes)*

Christians agree that God created the earth, but they sometimes hold different views about how the creation accounts in Genesis relate to scientific discoveries.

Option 1:

Q: What different views on creation have you come across?

Option 2:

Q: What thoughts have you had about this subject yourself? Discuss or take some time to think and write them down.

To help your discussion:

- *You could use the Briefing Sheet: Views on Genesis 1 if you need help thinking of some.*
- *You might want to go back to the question, 'How do you view science and faith?' from Session 1.*
- *You could return to these at the end of the session, if you use Epilogue Option 3*

Watch *Test of Faith* Part 2 – Chapters 1 and 2 *(25–35 minutes)*

In this part of the documentary we cover several different views on creation. You might want to mention this, and get people prepared to evaluate the different arguments for each position.

Use the chapter menu to play the first two chapters of Part 2 of the DVD. Pause the DVD at the end of each chapter using the cues below (press pause after you hear the cue).

Chapter 1 – Narrator: 'For Young Earth Creationism and Intelligent Design, then, Darwinian evolution is an enemy to faith.'
[Time code: 10 min. 05]
Chapter 2 – Narrator: 'This marriage of Darwin's theory and faith is known as Theistic Evolution.' [Time code: 14 min. 33]

*But if your group members are quite familiar with Young Earth Creationism and Intelligent Design, we suggest you watch through to the end of Chapter 2, without pausing for discussion.

**In-depth Session 2.2 discusses the science of Chapter 2.

After each chapter take a few minutes (depending on the size of your group) to help people process what they have just seen. For general discussion use an open question such as:

- What was new or most interesting for you?
- What did you find most surprising or challenging?
- What do you think the main messages were?
- What do you think? Do you agree?

Or you could use the Short Questions below.

Short Questions:

Chapter 1

Q: **What were the two different views that were presented on creation so far? (There is a third coming in the next chapter.)**

A1: There is *no* good evidence for an earth hundreds of millions of years old. If you want to take the Bible seriously you should believe what it says about the earth being created in six days.

A2: That there are signs of intentional design in creation.

Chapter 2

Q: **What is the third view on creation?**

A3: That evolution can fit within a Christian framework. This is called 'Theistic Evolution' or 'Evolutionary Creationism'.

Q: **What's a metaphysical framework? What does that have to do with a scientific concept like evolution?**

A: A metaphysical framework is a set of ideas through which we understand how the world works. Everyone works within a metaphysical framework of guiding ideas in life – and that can include religious and philosophical views such as Christianity or atheism, that are impossible to test by experiment. Simon Conway Morris thinks that evolutionary biology is compatible with several metaphysical frameworks, but that the one that makes the best sense is Christianity.

These ideas were covered in Session 1 (in the Discussion Topic 'How do people see the world?') and in Bonus Session 1b (in the Introduction Option 1: 'What questions does science answer?').

Glossary	
DNA	The chemical molecule inside every cell of every living thing that carries the instructions for its growth and development.
Intelligent Design	The idea that some parts of living things are too complex to have evolved, coupled with the idea that the information contained in DNA cannot have arisen by a process describable in purely material terms, so providing evidence for 'design'.
Theistic Evolution (or Evolutionary Creationism)	The belief that God created life through the process of evolution.
Young Earth Creationism	The belief that Genesis should be interpreted as a literal, historical and scientific account, and therefore that God created the world between 6,000 and 10,000 years ago in six twenty-four hour days.

SESSION 2

See page 29 of the **Study Guide**

Discussion Topics (45–55 minutes)

Use the three sections 'Genesis 1', 'Interpreting Genesis' and 'What's the Bottom Line?'. The other two are optional.

 **Genesis 1**   *Level: Intermediate*

Read Genesis 1.

> **Q1: What are the most important messages of this passage? What does it say about God? About God's relationship with the universe? About God's relationship with people?**
>
> *Hints:*
> - *There is one God.*
> - *God existed before creation.*
> - *God is the 'first cause' of creation, the reason creation exists.*
> - *God actively created the world.*
> - *God is independent of creation and has complete power over it.*
> - *God cares about creation.*
> - *What God created is good.*
> - *We are made in God's image.*
> - *God cares about us.*
> - *We care for creation at God's command.*

> **Q2: What part does the timescale have to play in thinking about the main messages in Genesis 1?**
>
> *Note:*
> *Some might think that the timescale of six days is important and some may not. It's still worth highlighting that it is a secondary issue, and that therefore it's possible for Christians to hold different views.*

 **Interpreting Genesis**   *Level: Easy*

Read the Briefing Sheet: Views on Genesis 1.

There are many different interpretations of Genesis 1, but the Briefing Sheet outlines three of the most widely-held views. Many of the other views are variations of these.

> **Q: Which of these views have you come across before?**
>
> *To help your discussion:*
> - *These could be divided into more specific categories, but for the purposes of this course this Briefing Sheet keeps things as simple as possible.*
> - *Because there is some overlap between these views, the Venn diagram should help to clarify this.*
> - *To encourage people to consider them with fresh eyes the Briefing Sheet doesn't label the different views, but if you want to make a connection to the documentary, view 1 is 'Young Earth Creationism', view 2 is the 'Day-Age' interpretation, and view 3 is 'Theistic Evolution', or 'Evolutionary Creationism'. Intelligent Design theory makes no claim to be a religious view, but it is compatible with certain forms of all three of these views.*
> - *If it's appropriate, ask the group which view they most readily identify with and why.*
> - *Perhaps some people will be torn between different views.*
> - *If you have time to go through the following two discussion sections, you could return to this section at the end and see if people's positions have been clarified or have shifted.*

(?) A Deeper Meaning

Level: Intermediate

View 3 on the Briefing Sheet: Views on Genesis 1 says that Genesis 1 is a piece of literature that describes a real event in non-scientific language.

Q1: Can you give any examples of stories in the Bible that have a deeper meaning?

Hint:
The obvious examples are the parables that Jesus told.

Q2: Can you give an example of a story being used in the Bible to explain a real event?

Hint:
If people can't think of any examples, you could read a couple of these:

- *2 Samuel 12:1–7b: the prophet Nathan tells King David a story about a lamb to get him to think about his adultery with Bathsheba.*
- *Ezekiel 17:1–4: Judah is the vine, and the king of Babylon (the first eagle) had made an agreement with the king of Judah that they would not rise up against him. However, Judah turned to Egypt (the second eagle) for military assistance with the result that the top classes from Judah were taken into exile to the east in Babylon.*
- *Genesis 37:2–11; 44:14: Joseph's symbolic dream of what will happen in the future.*
- *Hosea 11:1–4: God tells the story of the exodus by comparing Israel to a small child God is raising.*

Q3: What do you think of the idea that Genesis 1 might also have a deeper meaning?

(?) A Question of Days

Level: Intermediate

How long are the days in Genesis 1:
- Actual twenty-four hour days? (view 1)
- Long periods of time? (view 2)
- Symbolic of God's act of creation? (view 3)

Q1: How many different uses of the word 'day' are there in English?

Hint:
For example: 'in my day', 'in five days', 'the present day', 'my working day is 8 hours', 'in those days'.

Read Genesis 2:4; Exodus 16:30; Deuteronomy 28:33; Joel 1:15; and 2 Peter 3:8.

Q2: What are the different uses of the word 'day' in these passages? Can you think of any more?

Note: The Hebrew word *yom* has the same meanings as 'day' in English, but in Hebrew there isn't another word for an extended but fixed period of time (e.g., in English we have 'epoch', 'era' and 'age' as well as 'day').

To help your discussion:
- *Genesis 2:4: 'In the day …' (referring to the whole act of creation). You will need to look at a more literal translation, such as the NKJ or ESV. Because this doesn't refer to a 24-hour day, the NIV translates the verse differently.*
- *Exodus 16:30: 'So the people rested on the seventh day'.*
- *Deuteronomy 28:33: '… you will have nothing but cruel oppression all your days'.*
- *Joel 1:15: 'For the day of the Lord is near; it will come like destruction from the Almighty.'*
- *2 Peter 3:8: '… a day is like a thousand years, and a thousand years are like a day'.*

> ### Q3: Look at Genesis 1 again. What do you think the 'six days' mean in this passage?
>
> **To help your discussion:**
> - *The use of 'morning and evening' seems to say that in this passage we're talking about a 24-hour period of time – but with no sun and moon until day 4, what is the intended meaning of these words?*
> - *The last day doesn't end (Genesis 2:2–3). This is important for the theology of Hebrews 4:1–13 and Jesus refers to this concept when he explains his healing on the Sabbath (John 5:17).*

(?) **What's the Bottom Line?** *Level: Easy*

> ### Q: Think back to your answers to Q1 in the 'Genesis 1' Discussion Topic above. Did any of your discussion in the other sections contradict the core messages of Genesis?
>
> **Hint:**
> - *You should hear some interesting insights, but no real contradictions to the main messages identified. We return to the idea that this is a secondary issue, so it's possible for Christians to hold different views.*

Epilogue *(10–15 minutes)*

Discussions about creation are important, but they're not the end of the story.

" When we go back to Genesis … God doesn't give us the command, "Get everything right about the age of the earth, or exactly what happens in biology" … The command we have is to look after the earth, to be good stewards of the earth, to care for the earth in the right kind of way.

Dr Denis Alexander [Time code: 28 min. 42]

Read Genesis 1:26–28 and Genesis 2:15.

Bonus Session 2b will consider the environment and the evidence for climate change, but the clear principle is that we are to 'steward' God's creation.

Option 1:

Use the passages above to begin a time of prayer focusing on our role as stewards of God's creation and the part scientists have to play in this.

Option 2:

Take a map of the world, and pray through any difficult situations that you know about in different countries at the moment.

Option 3:

Hand out blank paper and pens, and make a note of:

1. Anything new you have learned – or opinions that have changed
2. Any conclusions you have come to
3. Any questions you still have
4. Things you'll do to find answers

You could plan in a session where you come back together to talk about what you've found out, and whether your answers to 1–4 have changed. Pray together for inspiration and clarity.

Option 4:

If you would like to sing, you could use one of the songs or hymns on the list in Appendix 3 on page 113.

See page 69 for the 'Taking it Further' list.

In-depth Session 2.2: An Accident in the Making?

Planning

Aim

The aim of this section is to begin to demystify the process of evolution and explore how it might be compatible with Christianity. There is also a surprise in store, because we will be presenting the evidence for purpose in this supposedly 'random chance' process.

As in Session 1, the goal is to engage with mainstream science and to ask: What are believing scientists encountering every day in their research? How could we think about these issues as Christians? Even if the jury is out for your group on how to interpret Genesis, it is important to know how Christians working in science are dealing with these issues in the light of their faith.

Some suggestions for a 1 ½ – 2 hour session:

	Basic introduction	In-depth	Big picture	A group with a lot of scientific knowledge
Introduction Option	any	1 or 2	1 or 2	3
DVD	✓	✓	✓	✓
It's a Process	✓	✓	✓	
What a Waste?				✓
Animal Death	choose one		✓	
A Random Process?	✓	✓	✓	✓
Is there Purpose in Evolution?		✓		✓
Epilogue Option	any	any	any	any

To split into two shorter sessions *(40–60 minutes each)*

Ask the group to read the material related to this session in the *Study Guide* beforehand.

First half-session:
- Introduction activity in pairs *(5–10 minutes)*
- DVD – watch *(8 minutes)* and discuss for 5–10 minutes after each chapter
- Epilogue *(5–10 minutes)*

Second half-session:
- Quick recap by leader *(5 minutes)*
- Discussion Topics – pick two or three that raised the most interest, or split into smaller groups to discuss different topics
- Epilogue *(5–10 minutes)*

Preparation for Participants *(optional):*
Thinking about evolution

For an introduction to evolution from a Christian perspective, read:

Denis R. Alexander, 'Is Evolution Atheistic?'
http://cis.thevirtualchurch.co.uk/assets/files/Resources/Articles/Article-Archive/evolution_atheistic.htm (introductory)

or

Simon Conway Morris, 'Extraterrestrials: Aliens like Us?'
http://adsabs.harvard.edu/abs/2005A&G....46d..24M (a paper about evolution)

Introduction

All of these questions lead people into thinking about evolution and how believing scientists hold evolutionary biology alongside Christian faith.

Option 1:

Q: Can you think of something in your life that seemed chaotic or random to you at the time, but made sense afterwards?

Option 2:

Q: Thinking back, can you identify a period in your life when, through a long process, you believe God was slowly teaching you something?

Option 3:

Q: What experiences have you had that made you stop and think about the incredible variety of living things in the world?

Watch *Test of Faith* Part 2 – Chapters 2 and 3 *(25–35 minutes)*

Use the chapter menu to play Chapters 2 and 3 of Part 2 of the DVD. Pause the DVD at the end of each chapter using the cues below (press pause after you hear the cue).

Chapter 2 – Narrator: 'This marriage of Darwin's theory and faith is known as Theistic Evolution.' [Time code: 14 min. 33]
Chapter 3 – Simon Conway Morris: '… are they themselves in any way congruent with those world pictures?'
[Time code: 18 min. 27]

After each chapter take a few minutes (depending on the size of your group) to help people process what they have just seen. For general discussion use an open question such as:

- What was new or most interesting for you?
- What did you find most surprising or challenging?
- What do you think the main messages were?
- What do you think? Do you agree?

Or you could use the Short Questions below.

Short Questions:

Chapter 2

Q: What is the third view on creation?
A: That evolution can fit within a Christian framework. This is called 'Theistic Evolution', or 'Evolutionary Creationism'.

Q: What's a metaphysical framework? What does that have to do with a scientific concept like evolution?

A: A 'metaphysical framework' is a set of ideas through which we understand the way the world works. Everyone works within a 'metaphysical framework' of guiding ideas in life – and that can include religious and philosophical views such as Christianity or atheism, that are impossible to test by experiment. Simon Conway Morris thinks that evolutionary biology is compatible with several metaphysical frameworks, but that the one that makes the best sense is Christianity.

Session 1 (in the Discussion Topic 'How do people see the world?') and Session 1b (in the Introduction Option 1: 'What questions does science answer?') cover these ideas.

Chapter 3

Q: What are the two meanings of the word 'random' that Ard Louis describes?

A1: In day-to-day life we use it to mean 'purposeless'.

A2: In a scientific sense it means that the microscopic details of a process may be unpredictable, but the overall process may be very predictable.

Q: Which meaning does he say fits with evolution?

A: The second.

Glossary	
chromosome	Each DNA strand in a living cell is wound up tightly into a chromosome. Depending on how human chromosomes are visualized in the lab, they can sometimes look like 'x' shapes or pairs of stripy socks.
genetics	The study of inherited characteristics and the variation of inherited characteristics among populations.
Human Genome Project	The international project to 'read' the whole of the human DNA code (the genome).
nihilism	Lack of belief in the existence of morality or meaning in life.

What is Evolution?

1. There is a huge amount of variation in nature – you only need to think of dogs or cats to realize this.

2. Differences in genes (the DNA instruction manual that is in every cell of every living thing) cause a lot of this variation.

3. The differences are caused by very rare changes in the genes as they are passed on.

Most will not have any effect.

Some will make them sick.

A very few will make them healthier than ever before.

4. Some variations will be more successful than others – certain breeds of cat may have more kittens than others, especially in the wild.

5. These genetically more successful cats will pass on more copies of their genes.

6. Eventually these more successful families will build up a range of genetic differences and become so different that they will form a new species that cannot breed with any animals outside of their own group.

SESSION 2

Discussion Topics *(45–55 minutes)*

Pick two or three to discuss.

This section could be used to focus mainly on plant and animal evolution. If you want to tackle specific questions of human evolution, use In-depth Session 2.3.

(?) It's a Process

Level: Intermediate

The history that has been painted for us in the documentary is a very long process – the formation of the universe, our planet, and the life on it.

IF THE EARTH WERE ONE YEAR OLD

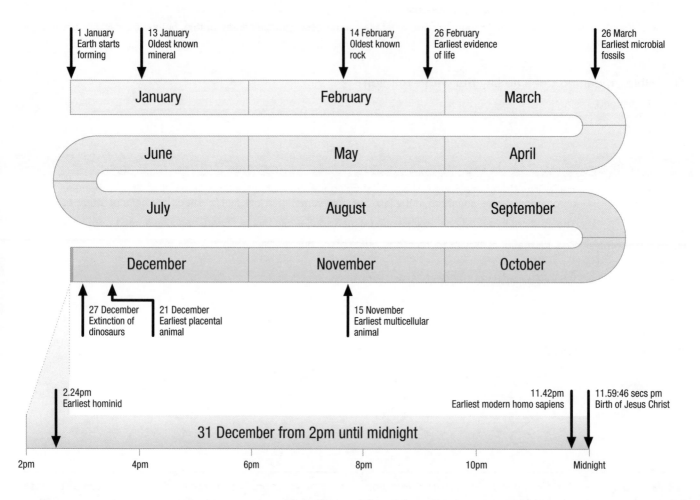

Copied with permission from D. Alexander and R.S. White, *Beyond Belief: Science, Faith and Ethical Challenges* (Lion, 2004), p. 98.

Why would God bother using such a long process when he could clearly create everything in an instant if he wanted to? Some people see a parallel between this process and the long history of the formation of Israel in the Old Testament and the spreading of the news about Jesus in the New Testament.

Q: Do you think this is justified? Think about what the Bible says about God's character and about your own experience.

Hints:

- *This links back to Introduction Option 2, if you used it.*

Points that suggest that God might work to create through a long process are:

- *God is patient.*
- *God often uses long processes to change things.*

Note: *We're not talking about process theology! God is outside of this process. We are the ones in the process.*

(?) What a Waste?

Level: Intermediate

" I think one of the biggest questions that many Christians find themselves wrestling with is, "**How can the process of evolution, with all its waste – or at least all its apparent waste – be reconciled with the idea of a loving God, a God who has purpose?**

Professor Alister McGrath [Time code: 18 min. 56]

Q1: What 'waste' do you see in the long process of creation that scientists propose?

Hints:

- *Many stars dying*
- *Many planets – only one earth*
- *Millions of species extinct*
- *Millions of seeds – one plant*
- *Millions of birds – not all survive to adulthood*
- *Millions of sperm – one person*

Q2: When you look at creation as a whole, rather than from the point of view of one individual bird, seed, species or star, what are some ways to view the long process besides as 'wasteful'? In other words, how could God (and how could we) value species that were extinct long before we came on the scene?

Hints:

- *Recycling*
- *Making materials that are needed – e.g., fertilizer, different environments, fossil fuels (used wisely!)*
- *A process of preparation for what's to come later*

Some more examples:

- The universe needed to be the size that it is to sustain our planet for a long enough period of time for life to develop and remain stable for even just a few thousand years.
- When a star explodes and dies, new elements are made that form new stars and planets. Our bodies were formed from the dust of planet earth, so we are made of stardust.
- Tectonic plates (the earth's outer crust) move and cause earthquakes and volcanoes. These bring up rich nutrients from the earth's core that are vital for sustaining life on our planet.

SESSION 2

These scientists see this process as part of God's generosity, or extravagance. The God who 'owns the cattle on a thousand hills' (Psalm 50:10) has made us a huge universe and a rich world!

> **Q3: Do you think it's justified to say that there would be no waste in a long process of creation?**

(?) Animal Death   *Level: Intermediate*

If God created using a process of evolution, this would mean that the death of many animals was involved. Could this really be part of God's original plan?

Read Genesis 4:3–7; Genesis 9:3; Job 38: 39–41; and Psalm 104:21.

> **Q1: What is God's attitude to animal death in the Bible? Is it different from human death?**
>
> *Hints:*
> - *God expects us to eat animals.*
> - *God provides food for animals – including the carnivorous ones.*

Read Genesis 1:30 and look at the Briefing Sheet: Views on Genesis 1.

> **Q2: How would different people interpret this verse? Who was eating what (or whom!)?**
>
> *Hints:*
> - *Views 1 and 3: On the third day God created the land and the plants to cover it. On the sixth day God gave the plants to the people and animals to eat. So people and animals were vegetarian before the fall.*
> - *View 2: Not all the animals eat only plants, some are carnivorous. Because this isn't a scientific account, it's there to make the point that God is providing for his creation.*

> **Q3: Which of these views do you think makes the most sense in the light of God's attitude to animals in the rest of the Bible (Q1)?**
>
> *To help your discussion:*
> - *Some may think that animal death was not God's original plan, in the same way that a man having several wives was tolerated but not part of God's original plan for people.*
> - *Animals are not moral creatures – there is nothing in the Bible to suggest that – and the death of a human is far more important than the death of an animal. See the section on human evolution in In-depth Session 2.3.*

(?) A Random Process?   *Level: Easy*

Dr Ard Louis said that the word 'random' can mean two things:
- In everyday life we use it to mean 'purposeless'.
- From a scientific way of thinking it means that the tiny details are unpredictable – while the overall process can still be very predictable.

And it's clear that evolution is the scientific type of random process: it acts as a 'random optimizer' to find the best solution to a problem. [Time code: 15 min. 04]

Read Proverbs 16:33 and Genesis 50:20.

Q1: Keeping the second definition of the word 'random' in mind, try to think of something in your past life that seemed chaotic or random to you at the time, but made sense afterwards.

Think back to the introduction if you used that option.

Q2: What do you think of the idea that God might work in creation in a similar way?

In answering Q1 people may have already mentioned some events that involved God interacting with (the non-human part of) creation. If God is interacting with creation in this way, then could he have been working in the same way in creation before we were on the scene?

Q3: Is it possible that God could be in control of a process like evolution?

The answer may be 'yes, but …' and people will almost certainly have more questions. The main question we are dealing with here is whether God could potentially work through a seemingly random process like evolution.

(?) **Is there Purpose in Evolution?**   *Level: In-depth*

Read the Briefing Sheet: Is there Purpose in Evolution?

" But is this another scientist claiming science can prove God?

" Emphatically I would not say, here's convergence, this is a proof of … anything in fact. **It merely says that the world is structured, and then you must stand back from that position and say, "Well, why is the world structured in the way it is?"** And if there are claims made by particular religious traditions, are they themselves in any way congruent with those world pictures?

Professor Simon Conway Morris [Time code: 18 min. 03]

Q: Do you think this view of the world fits with a Christian belief in a God who intentionally created a world and the people in it? Why or why not?

Epilogue

Pick one of the options that you didn't use in Session 2.1.

See page 69 for the 'Taking it Further' list.

In-depth Session 2.3: Evolution, Suffering and the Fall

Planning

Aim

The aim of this section is to look at some of the most challenging questions raised by the discussion of creation in the DVD, and Theistic Evolution in particular. These are questions that many theologians and biblical scholars are still working hard to address, so the aim here is simply to show where the debate is for Christians, what the common ground is, and then to open it up for discussion so that people can begin to think about these issues for themselves.

The sections on human evolution and the fall are based, with permission, on the book by Dr Denis Alexander, *Creation or Evolution: Do We Have to Choose?*

Our principle in coming to this session is [for 'who Adam and Eve were', substitute any scientific question]:

" To find out who Adam and Eve were, **we need to start with the biblical text**. We do not start with the evolutionary narrative and then try and impose it on the biblical text, but rather do the reverse – **listen to what the Bible has to say and then see whether there are any interesting resonances with the evolutionary account**.

> Dr Denis Alexander, *Creation or Evolution: Do We Have to Choose?* (p. 191)

In this session the epilogue is particularly important because it provides a chance to move the discussion away from secondary issues and back to common ground for Christians. It will also help people to focus on the present and how we are to live here and now in this fallen world.

Some suggestions for a 1 ½ – 2 hour session:

Note: This session isn't suitable for groups who would like a basic introduction, so we have not included any options for this in the planning table.

	In-depth	Big picture	A group with a lot of scientific knowledge
Introduction Option	any	any	any
DVD	✓	✓	✓
Human Evolution			
The Fall	Try to work through all three, but if time is short choose one.		
Suffering			
Epilogue Option	any	any	any

To split into two shorter sessions *(40–60 minutes each)*

Ask the group to read the material relating to this session in the *Study Guide* beforehand.

First half-session:

- Introduction activity in pairs *(5–10 minutes)*
- DVD – watch *(9 minutes)* and discuss 5–10 minutes afterwards
- Discussion Topics – start one
- Epilogue *(5–10 minutes)*

Second half-session:

- Quick recap by leader *(5 minutes)*
- DVD – watch again if necessary *(9 minutes)*
- Discussion Topics – finish the one you started in the first half-session
- Epilogue *(5–10 minutes)*

Preparation for Participants *(optional)*:
Thinking about evolution

As background reading for this session, read:

Graeme Finlay, '*Homo divinus:* The Ape that Bears God's Image'
www.scienceandchristianbelief.org/articles/finlay.pdf

or

Explore the following web page, looking in particular for information about different views on the creation of humans:
The American Scientific Affiliation's 'Creation and Evolution' page (different views from a Christian perspective)
www.asa3.org/ASA/topics/Evolution/index.html

Introduction *(10–15 minutes)*

Discuss or write down your answers to one of these questions:

Option 1:

Q: Five-year-olds are great at asking unanswerable questions. What are the most difficult questions you've heard someone ask?

Option 2:

Q: What do you think is the hardest 'big question' about the world?

Option 3:

Q: What, for you, is the most important unanswered question that this course has raised so far?

Watch *Test of Faith* Part 2 – Chapter 4 *(15–20 minutes)*

Use the chapter menu to play Chapter 4 of Part 2 of the DVD. Pause the DVD at the end of the chapter using the cue below (press pause after you hear the cue).

Chapter 4 – Alister McGrath: '… and until science confronts that enigma, we're stuck.' [Time code: 26 min. 00]

Take a few minutes (depending on the size of your group) to help people process what they have just seen. For general discussion use an open question such as:

- What was new or most interesting for you?
- What did you find most surprising or challenging?
- What do you think the main messages were?
- What do you think? Do you agree?

Or you could use the Short Questions below.

Short Questions:

Chapter 4

Q: **The biggest challenge to faith that comes from evolution is the role of suffering and death in the process. How do the two scientists in this chapter of *Test of Faith* answer that challenge?**

A: Both agree that it is a difficult question and that there is not a completely satisfactory answer.

John Polkinghorne thinks that it is a more positive thing for a loving God to make a creation that can 'make itself', than for God to simply make it (and us) with no freedom, and therefore no opportunity for evil. It may be 'an inescapable shadow side' that comes from creation being able to produce life.

Francis Collins thinks that this may be the only way to make a good and stable universe for us to live in.

Q: **What is the source of hope that Alister McGrath's first comment gives us?**

A: The New Testament tells us that this was not the ultimate plan for our lives – the physically strong will not triumph over the weak.

Glossary	
the fall	The account of how people became disobedient to God.
germ cells	Eggs and sperm.
malignant	Bad or harmful, often used with regards to cancer; the opposite of benign (harmless).
mutation	A change in the DNA code that happens during the life cycle of a living thing. Mutations can be caused by a toxic chemical or other environmental disturbance, or by a mistake in copying the DNA when new cells are made.
somatic cells	All the cells in the body except eggs and sperm.

Discussion Topics *(45–60 minutes)*

Unlike the other sessions, every topic below is at an 'in-depth' level.

(?) Human Evolution

Dr Francis Collins outlined the evidence for human evolution in Chapter 2 of Part 2 of the DVD. [Time code: 11 min. 03]

If he is right, this immediately raises two questions: 'Who were Adam and Eve?' and 'How are we special compared to other animals?'

Read Genesis 2: 4–25.

Q1: **What are the most important messages in this passage? What does it say about God? About God's relationship with the universe? About God's relationship with people?**

Hints:

- *People are made like the animals but are more than animals – one reason is because they have the breath/spirit (same word in Hebrew) of God (v. 7).*
- *God has provided us with everything we need (vv. 15–17).*
- *One of the things we need is relationship, and animals aren't enough (v. 18).*
- *God has called us to work in and care for creation (vv. 15, 19–20)*
- *Men and women need each other, and God intended monogamous (married) relationships (vv. 18–24).*

Read the Briefing Sheet: Views on Genesis 2 and 3, Who were Adam and Eve?

> **Q2: Which of these views do you think could fit best with the biblical and scientific account?**
>
> ***To help your discussion:***
>
> - *You could also use the Briefing Sheet: Views on Genesis 1 to find where these views come from in terms of interpreting Genesis 1. Which of the views on Adam and Eve could be compatible with each view on Genesis 1?*

So how are we special compared to other animals? The Bible says that we are made 'in God's image'. Bonus Session 3b will explore the implications of this further, but for now we are interested in how that came to be. There are several ways to see this:

1. We were specially created as we are – evolution had no part to play

2. God took evolved *Homo sapiens* and chose them to bear his image by divine fiat.

3. There was a growing spiritual awareness in *Homo sapiens*.

For all three views, there is a point of coming into relationship with God. The image of God is something God gives to us and has nothing to do with our own abilities.

It would be impossible to know the details for any of these possibilities but whatever happened, at least as far as positions 2 and 3 are concerned, at some point a pair or group of creatures came into personal relationship with God.

> **Q3: Which of the three 'image of God' views, above, fit to which 'Who were Adam and Eve?' views on the Briefing Sheet? What do you think of these views and how they fit the biblical account?**
>
> ***Hints:***
>
> - *View 1 fits A and B.*
> - *View 2 fits C, D and E.*
> - *View 3 fits C, D and E.*

> **Q4: There are many views on the interpretation of Genesis 2 (discussed above). Did any of your discussion complement or contradict the main messages of Genesis 2 that were discussed in Q1?**
>
> ***Note:***
>
> *You will probably hear some interesting insights but no real contradictions to the main messages people picked out. We return to the idea that this is a secondary issue, so it's possible for Christians to hold different views.*

SESSION 2

? The Fall

The aim of this section is to look at the doctrine of the fall and relate it to the interpretation of Genesis and science. The question is: How does the fall relate to suffering and death in the world? The Discussion Topic on suffering, below, will examine this particular question in more depth.

" Our fall, therefore, is … [our] falling out of God's purposes for humanity, a refusal to be what God made us to be, a turning away of a summons and a calling to reflect God back to himself in our dealings with him and with one another.

Tom Smail, *Like Father, Like Son: The Trinity Imaged in our Humanity* (Paternoster, 2005), p. 213

Read Genesis 3:1–24.

Q1: How were Adam and Eve disobedient? What are the consequences of their sin? What can we learn about God from his response?

Hints:

- *They were created in the image of God, but by wanting to 'be like God' they tried to replace him (vv. 1–6).*
- *They were supposed to reflect God – they were 'clothed' with his glory – but by trying to replace him, they became truly naked (vulnerable), and they were ashamed (vv. 7–10).*
- *God describes the consequences that will follow from their sin (vv. 14–19).*
- *God is gracious and will still use them for their created purpose (v. 20), he cares for them in their fallenness (v. 21), and he will not have them live forever with the consequences of their sin (vv. 22–24). Rather, they will die and be redeemed to new, sinless life by Christ.*

The Bible talks about three types of death:

- Physical death (Genesis 25:8)
- Spiritual death (Colossians 2:13)
- Eternal spiritual death, or second death (Matthew 10:28)

Q2: Which type of death do you think resulted from Adam and Eve's disobedience? When or how did it happen?

This is a key part of the fall narrative, and details like this will help to focus the discussion in the following question.

Read the second half of the Briefing Sheet: Views on Genesis 2 and 3, Views on the fall.

Q3: Which of these views do you think could fit best with the biblical account?

To help your discussion:

- *The question of whether two people were involved in this event becomes much more important.*
- *But having defined the most important messages of the passage in the answer to Q1, these discussions should be interesting but not threatening to anyone's faith.*
- *This question may well raise the issue of suffering. If you feel your discussion has come to the point of focusing on suffering and you don't have time to do another Discussion Topic, you could suggest tackling the following section in a future session and move on to the Epilogue.*

(?) Suffering

This section deals with the question of 'physical evil'. Evil caused by human sinfulness is obviously a result of the fall, but what about other sorts of evil? Science is telling us that death, natural disasters and disease have been present in the world since the beginning. How are Christians who accept evolution able to reconcile this with the biblical account?

" The consequences of the evolutionary process are, admittedly, at times things that cause suffering for individuals even today. A child with cancer may well be seen as one of those side-effects of the fact that DNA copying is not perfect, **it's important that DNA copying not be perfect or evolution wouldn't be possible, but if it results in a cancer arising in a child, isn't that a terrible price to pay**? These are difficult questions to be sure.

Dr Francis Collins, [Time code: 21 min. 03]

" **Why would a loving God allow a tsunami that would kill hundreds of thousands of people?** There are various explanations; I'm not sure that any of them are completely satisfactory. This is one of the toughest questions that believers have to face.

Dr Francis Collins, [Time code: 23 min. 34]

" There is a great danger in tackling this kind of topic that the discussion might seem demeaning to someone personally going through a period of suffering … these are not the kind of reflections that are likely to be of much help to someone actually passing through a period of suffering (although they might be), but I think they do have pastoral significance in preparing us for times when we will experience suffering in the future.

Dr Denis Alexander, *Creation or Evolution: Do We Have to Choose?* (p. 277)

Q1: How would you define 'physical evil'? How is it different from any other kind of evil?

Hints:

- *We call things 'physical evil' that happen to us that cause us to experience pain and suffering, and are not caused by human sinfulness.*
- *There is a fuzzy line between what we're calling 'physical evil' and the evil that human sinfulness causes. How can you tell whether any particular experience of pain and suffering is caused by human sinfulness or not? We come to this in Q4.*

Q2: What are the possible explanations for the existence of 'physical evil'?

Hint:

- *There are only two real possibilities: either it was always there in creation, or it happened as a consequence of the fall.*

Q3: In Genesis 1:31 God says that the world is 'very good'. Do you think this could include the death and extinction of many species?

To help your discussion:

- *People will probably begin to ask what 'good' means. Is it 'perfect' or is it 'fit for purpose'?*
- *God commanded Adam and Eve to subdue the earth. Would this apply to a perfect world? There was obviously some work to be done. (If you look in a concordance for other places where the Hebrew word for 'subdue' is used, it refers to subduing a rebellious nation.)*

How could pain and suffering be part of God's original plan for us in a world God declared to be 'good'? There are several possible ways of looking at this:

1. Would physical suffering have been experienced as evil before the fall?
2. Would people have been protected from physical suffering in the Garden of Eden?
3. What if the good world was not meant to be a paradise, but the place where people are made ready for eternal life in the new creation?

Q4: What do you think? Do you think that Adam and Eve, even if they didn't die, would have experienced pain and suffering?

To help your discussion:

- *Death is not discussed here – it is a separate issue and dealt with in the previous section, 'The Fall'.*

Read Revelation 21:1–4.

Q5: What is God's ultimate purpose for creation?

Hint:

- *God's ultimate purpose is to be with the created world, and that the world will be with him forever (vv. 1–3). Because God is with us, and we are with God, there will be no more suffering or evil (v. 4).*

SESSION 2

Epilogue *(10–15 minutes)*

Option 1: A response to the question of suffering

What, ultimately, is God's response to the question of suffering? Two answers are given. Read the passages and use them as the basis for a time of discussion, quiet reflection or prayer

Job 38:1–7 and Isaiah 55:9

God is in control, and suffering is something we cannot fully understand for the moment. Perhaps we cannot answer the question of suffering on human terms or judge God by our standards. As the book of Job makes clear, who are we to try to hold God to account? Whatever the answer is, it will be ultimately consistent with God's character as revealed in Scripture.

John 11:32–36; Luke 23:33–43; and Revelation 21:3–5.

The gospel. God came to us in the person of Jesus Christ and shared in our suffering. On the cross God was at the mercy of the worst humanity could offer, in addition to experiencing the worst that humanity deserves. In the resurrection Jesus triumphed over death and instigated a new creation which, when it comes to full fruition, will be a place where pain and suffering are abolished. This is the hope we have in the present situation. The Bible's final words on suffering are about the new creation.

Option 2: A higher ethic

We are not called to take our ethics from the animals, with their interactions that are a complex mixture of competition and care, but from the Bible.

" One of the points I'd like to make here is this. As I read the New Testament, I see a whole series of value statements that are completely opposed to Darwinism. It is not the strong who will triumph, it's actually the weak, and so on. And the key point here is that maybe **the gospel actually is saying to us that we need to articulate a system of values which contradict those that we see in nature around us**, that the way nature behave is not the way things are meant to be, that just because species are in competition we don't need to be in competition with each other. It's about a higher ethic than that.

Professor Alister McGrath [Time code 22 min. 27]

Read Philippians 2:1–11 and use it as a starter for a time of quiet reflection and prayer.

Option 3: Compassion and healing

Part of what God calls us to do is to be compassionate to each other. Jesus models this compassion and illustrates it in the story of 'the good Samaritan' (Luke 10:25–37). Medicine, science and technology are an extension of that desire to be compassionate and 'subdue the earth and rule over it'.

Pray for people who are working in these areas. (You could look up one of the organizations listed in the 'Taking it Further' section in Session 3 (page 90) if you would like to pray for a specific issue in medicine.)

Option 4:

If you would like to sing, you could use one of the songs or hymns on the list in Appendix 3 on page 113.

Taking it Further

Websites and articles to download on creation:

Bob White, 'The Age of the Earth'
www.st-edmunds.cam.ac.uk/faraday/resources/Faraday%20Papers/Faraday%20Paper%208%20White_EN.pdf

Ernest Lucas, 'Interpreting Genesis in the 21st Century'
www.st-edmunds.cam.ac.uk/faraday/resources/Faraday%20Papers/Faraday%20Paper%2011%20Lucas_EN.pdf

Graeme Finlay, '*Homo divinus:* The Ape that Bears God's Image'
www.scienceandchristianbelief.org/articles/finlay.pdf

The American Scientific Affiliation's 'Creation and Evolution' page (different views from a Christian perspective)
www.asa3.org/ASA/topics/Evolution/index.html

Answers in Genesis (Young Earth Creationism): **www.answersingenesis.org**

The Discovery Institute (Intelligent Design): **www.discovery.org**

Reasons to Believe (The day-age view): **www.reasons.org**

Books on creation:

Deborah B. Haarsma and Loren D. Haarsma, *Origins: A Reformed Look at Creation, Design and Evolution* (Faith Alive Christian Resources, 2007). This is a very approachable introduction to the area of science and faith, and creation. It examines the origins of the universe and living things. Further material is available on **www.faithaliveresources/origins**, including questions that can be used by a small reading group. The book covers a range of views.

Norman Geisler (ed.), *The Genesis Debate: Three Views on the Days of Creation* (Crux Press, 2001). Three pairs of authors present different views on the days of creation: the 24-hour view, the day-age views, and the framework view, and respond to each other's writing.

Paul Nelson, Robert C. Newman and Howard J. Van Till, *Three Views on Creation and Evolution* (ed. John Mark Reynolds and J.P. Moreland; Zondervan, 1999). Proponents of Young Earth Creationism, Old Earth Creationism and Theistic Evolution each present their different views, explain why the controversy is important and describe the interplay between their understandings of science and theology. Various scholars critique each view.

David Wilkinson, *The Message of Creation* (The Bible Speaks Today; IVP, 2002). This is a very thorough look at the themes of creation throughout the Bible, beginning with Genesis 1–3. The following sections deal with: the songs of creation that praise our Creator God; Jesus' relationship to creation; the lessons the writers of the Bible teach using creation; and the new creation.

Ernest Lucas, *Can We Believe Genesis Today?* (IVP, 2005). This book explains how scholars have interpreted Genesis 1–11, historically and in the light of modern science. Lucas looks at various interpretations, noting the problems with each and giving sources for further reading. He highlights his own view, that mainstream science and the Bible are compatible.

Denis Alexander, *Creation or Evolution: Do We Have to Choose?* (Monarch, 2008). This is an in-depth look at all the questions concerning creation and evolution, from the perspective of Theistic Evolution.

Darrel Falk, *Coming to Peace with Science* (IVP [USA], 2004). Darrel Falk sympathetically picks his way through the various theological arguments on all sides of the debate and comes to the conclusion that Christianity is compatible with evolutionary biology.

Bonus Session 2b: The Environment

Planning

Aim

The aim of this session is to expand on the material in Part 2 of the documentary that focused on the environment and to move through several questions: What is the problem? Why should we bother about it? And how does that fit into God's plan for the earth?

Although people will have a chance to discuss the evidence for global warming, the assumption here is that the scientific evidence for climate change is overwhelming and is just one part of the environmental damage that has been done, and is being done, to the world.

This all comes within the framework of creation, fall and redemption. Caring for the environment is not an alternative to the gospel but is part of our God-given responsibility to care for the world. It's a responsibility the whole church needs to take seriously, not just a few extra-motivated Christians, and there are many ways we can get involved.

The aim is not to leave people feeling hopeless or overwhelmed. This is not an unsolvable issue; there is real hope that we can help to reduce the effects of environmental damage and take better care of God's world.

The 'Taking it Further' list, page of activities, and lifestyle audit will help people find out more and take further action.

Equipment needed
- You will need to use the DVD bonus interviews for this session. See the 'bonus features' section of the DVD for details.
- A large piece of paper, whiteboard or flip chart if you wish to use Q2 in the Discussion Topic 'Environmental Issues' as a group activity.

Some suggestions for a 1 ½ – 2 hour session:

	Basic introduction	In-depth	Big picture	A group with a lot of knowledge on the environment
Introduction Option	5	2	3 or 4	any
Environmental Issues	✓	✓	✓ (Q2 & Q4)	
God's Purpose for Creation	✓	✓	✓	✓
The Putrefied World		✓	✓	✓
The Purified World	✓	✓	✓	✓
What Do We Do?	✓	✓	✓	✓
Epilogue Option	1	1	2 or 3	1

To split into two shorter sessions *(40–60 minutes each)*

Ask the group to read the material relating to this session in the *Study Guide* beforehand.

First half-session:
- Introduction activity in pairs *(5–10 minutes)*
- Discussion Topics – pick one or two
- Epilogue *(5–10 minutes)*

Second half-session:
- Quick recap by leader *(5 minutes)*
- Discussion Topics – pick one or two more
- Epilogue *(5–10 minutes)*

Preparation for Participants *(optional):*
The environment

This is an opportunity for people to look at climate change and at environmental issues in general – especially the evidence that there is a problem and that we can be involved in the solution.

Read one of the articles suggested on the 'Taking it Further' list, or the two Briefing Sheets for this session.

or

Keep an eye (or ear) out for stories in the media about the environment. What are the issues? Who do they affect? What solutions are suggested?

Introduction *(10–15 minutes)*

Option 1:

Ask people to describe a recent encounter with some aspect of God's creation that made them think, 'That's amazing!'

Option 2:

Read Psalm 104. What does this psalm tell us about the relationship between God, people and creation?

Hint:
- *God is the Creator and sustainer of everything. We are part of creation and depend on God, just as every other living thing also depends on God.*

Option 3:

Put a glass of water in the middle of the room. Ask people to reflect on what this calls to mind about creation.

Hints:
- *The nature of God (it's symbolic of living water, etc.)*
- *Bible passages (e.g., John 4:10–15; Revelation 21:6)*
- *Practical realities (e.g., water treatment/chemicals, problems in other countries)*
- *God's amazing creation*

Option 4:

Same as Option 3, but with a collection of natural objects – e.g., soil, leaf, stone, flame.

Option 5:

Use Discussion Topic: Environmental Issues, Q1 as an introductory activity.

Discussion Topics *(60–90 minutes)*

(?) **Environmental Issues** *Level: Intermediate / In-depth (if use options)*

This section will allow those who are not familiar with environmental issues to look at the evidence, especially for climate change, and think it through.

Q1: What have you heard, read or watched about the environment or environmental issues recently?

To help your discussion:

- *The purpose of this question is to draw out what people already know and get them thinking broadly about environmental issues.*
- *Try not to focus just on global warming – draw out other issues as well – but you could use the two climate change Briefing Sheets for Session 2 if there is a lot of confusion on that issue.*

Many of the issues we face are interconnected:

Water – provision of clean water for a growing population and problems caused by drought or floods

Climate change – A small increase in the overall temperature of the earth's atmosphere has a huge effect on the weather

Population[ii] – The population of the world has almost doubled in the last 40 years. How will everyone have enough food and water? (World population in 2005: 6,514,751; and in 1965: 3,342,771 – an increase of x1.95.)

Soil degradation – Overgrazing and deforestation mean that soil is washed from exposed land

Destruction of the places where living things usually grow (habitat loss), and a reduction in the number and variety of living things growing in the world (**reduced biodiversity**)

Q2: Can you map out how these things might be related?

To help your discussion:

- *It might be easiest to do this as a group on a large piece of paper or on a whiteboard or flipchart.*
- *There are plenty of different ways to draw this, but here is one:*

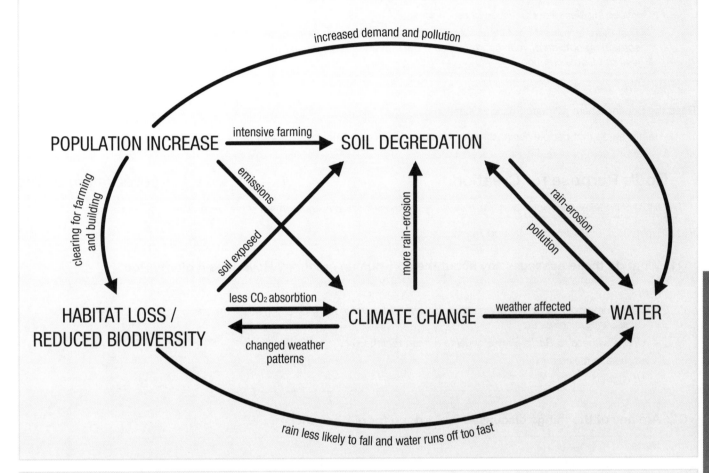

Q3: How seriously do you think we should take these issues, especially climate change?

To help your discussion:

- *The rest of the session should help with the answer to this question and give hope to those who might find this section depressing.*
- *There is some hype about the effects of global warming, so we have been careful to present scenarios based on the most accurate scientific predictions and to leave out any that are more speculative.*
- *You may find the Briefing Sheet: The Science behind Climate Change useful as it presents the scientific consensus.*
- *John Houghton explains in the clip referred to below how remarkable it is that so many scientists came together and agreed on the conclusions of the international investigation into the evidence for global climate change.*

(?) **Environmental Issues** *(Optional):*

▶ **Watch the bonus interview: 2.1 John Houghton** *(1 min. 45 sec.)*

The IPCC was an international panel set up by the by the World Meteorological Organization (WMO) and the United Nations Environment Programme (UNEP) to assess the scientific evidence for human-induced climate change.

Sir John Houghton was the chair or co-chair of the scientific assessment working group of the IPCC from 1988 until 2002.

> **Q4: What does the story in this clip say about John Houghton's experience as a scientist and a Christian?**
>
> *Hints:*
>
> - *There's no mention of conflict between the scientists.*
> - *Values in science are Christian ones – honesty.*
> - *That there is 'honest consensus' despite cultural and religious differences, as well as the idea of 'dealing with something outside of yourself', together show that there is scientific truth out there to be discovered. That truth is about God's creation*

Read the Briefing Sheet: Climate Change Questions.

Some do not agree that people cause climate change. The Briefing Sheet outlines some of these views, as well as a response.

? God's Purpose for Creation   *Level: Intermediate*

This section takes the focus away from ourselves and asks: What is creation really for? And what is our place in it?

Read Psalm 98:4–9; Psalm 19:1–4a; and Romans 1:20.

> **Q1: What do these passages say about the non-human creation? How does it glorify God?**
>
> *Hints:*
>
> - *Creation worships God. It brings glory to God and worships him by being itself: the sea by roaring, the trees by whispering/singing, etc.*
> - *It is a witness to God's glory alongside human testimony.*
> - *It reflects his creativity.*
> - *It is good.*

> **Q2: Are any of the things discussed in Q1 done for our benefit?**
>
> *Hints:*
>
> - *No, only the way that creation points us to God.*
> - *Creation is not just there for us to use, it also glorifies God and worships him on its own. This is the primary purpose of all of creation (including human beings).*

Read Genesis 1:26–30 and Genesis 2:15.

> **Q3: What is our status in relation to the rest of creation? What does God command us to do?**
>
> *Hints:*
>
> - *We are the only creatures who are made in God's image (Gen 1:27). (Bonus Session 3b will examine this further.)*
> - *God gives us the same things to eat as the other animals, so we have no special rights to consumption (Gen 1:30). (Note: we are not commanded to be vegetarians, see Gen. 9:3.)*
> - *God gives us dominion, which means we are given responsibility to care for creation, not to exploit it or have rights over it (Gen. 1:28).*
> - *God tells Adam to tend and care for the garden (Gen. 2:15). The Hebrew words here can be translated 'to serve and preserve'.*
> - *God released and blessed people to go into the world (Gen. 1:28, like a benediction at the end of a church service). NB: God also blessed and released the sea creatures (Gen. 1:22).*

The Putrefied World

Level: Easy

Why do we have environmental problems? Recognizing that we live in a fallen world answers that question.

Read the passages below and identify the chain of broken relationships in creation:

Genesis 3:8–11

- *Broken relationship with God*

Genesis 3:12–13

- *Broken relationships in marriage/between men and women.*

Genesis 3:15–19

- *Broken relationship with the rest of creation (enmity between women and animals, as well as between Adam and the ground)*

Genesis 4:3–9

- *Broken relationships in families*

Genesis 6:11–12

- *Continuing broken relationships within society*

 Watch the bonus interview: 2.2 John Houghton *(3 min.)*

 ## The Purified World

Level: In-depth

Why should we bother too much about looking after the world when it will have to come to an end at some point anyway? One answer involves the problems that environmental damage causes here and now, and especially for the poor, but there is also another reason, below.

Read Colossians 1:15–20.

Q1: What was and is Jesus' role in creation?

Hints:

- *Jesus is head of creation (Creator, sustainer, redeemer, gives purpose).*
- *He is restoring right order: the work of the cross is for creation, too – restoring its relationship with God.*

 Watch the bonus interview: 2.3 Alistair McGrath *(2 min. 30 sec.)*

Read Romans 8:19–23.

Q2: What will ultimately happen to the non-human creation?

Hint:

- *It will be renewed, which is connected to our resurrection.*

SESSION 2

Read 2 Peter 3:10–13.

> **Q3:** **If creation is renewed, what might the fire in this passage refer to?**
>
> ***To help your discussion:***
>
> • *There is a lot of discussion about this passage, but in the wider context of the Bible it makes the most sense if it's interpreted as judgement, purification and renewing – rather than as destruction and recreation. The Bible often uses the language of fire to talk about the judgement and purification of God's people (e.g., Malachi 3:2–3; 1 Peter 1:6–7).*
>
> • *It might help to look at Genesis 6:13. The flood didn't completely destroy the world.*

(?) What Do We Do?   *Level: Easy*

> **Q:** **With all the environmental problems that we face how can we have hope now, and for the future?**
>
> ***Hints:***
>
> • *Now: Colossians 1:15–20 says that Jesus has reconciled all things through his life, death and resurrection. Jesus has thereby restored the relationships with God that were broken at the fall. But, as we know, this restoration is a work in progress.*
>
> • *Future: Romans 8:19–23 and 2 Peter 3:10–13 say that this restoration will be completed 'in the day of the Lord' when we will receive our resurrection bodies and live in the 'new heaven and new earth'. Revelation 21 and 22 describe the new creation in figurative language.*

 Watch bonus interviews *(4 min. 15 sec.):* **2.4 Ian Hutchinson / 2.5 Catherine Cutler / 2.6 John Houghton**

• *These clips should leave people with a sense of hope and a sense that they can do something that has an impact.*

Epilogue *(10–15 minutes)*

Option 1:

Fill in Sheet 1: 'What on earth am I doing? A personal lifestyle audit'.

Option 2:

Use one of the following psalms as a basis for giving thanks as a group, with one-line prayers: Psalm 104; 148; 96; or 98.

Option 3:

Use one of the creation creeds or prayers from one of these sites:

www.livesimply.org.uk
www.ctbi.org.uk/339#additional

Option 4:

If you would like to sing, you could use one of the songs or hymns on the list in Appendix 3 on page 113.

Activities

You might want to take some extra time to do something as a group, or encourage people to arrange to do one of these activities together or with their families.

1. Cook a sustainable, local and seasonal fellowship meal

If food is grown locally it usually will not have been transported so far, especially if bought from a local shop. (Some of the larger chains will buy produce locally then ship it far away to have it packaged for less than it would cost locally!) From a purely culinary point of view, food bought from a local producer usually tastes much better. It can also be cheaper.

2. Make your garden bee and butterfly friendly

Make sure there is a source of water (a bird bath with a few twigs will do). Plant pollen- and nectar-rich plants. Many modern varieties of flowers don't produce very much pollen, but old varieties and wild roses work well. In order for plants to produce good nectar they need good soil, so making sure that it is just slightly acidic and has the right nutrition is important. A good way to do this is to dig in lots of fertilizer or mulch. Try not to use herbicides and pesticides, but if you must do check to make sure they are bee friendly. Plant flowers together instead of in small islands, and try to have plants that flower at different times of the year. Learn about local species habitats. For butterflies, plant the plants which they like to lay eggs on (and that become food for caterpillars). Plant shrubs for shelter and, if possible, some fruit-bearing trees or bushes.

3. Discussion

Have you ever heard a person being referred to as a 'consumer'? What is the difference between the words 'person' and 'consumer'? What does this say about our contemporary outlook? What's God's vision?

- You could make a list of things people are called in contemporary culture (e.g., person, consumer, agent, character, actor, steward).
- What do these things mean? How do they affect they way we view ourselves? What is God's view?

4. Go for a walk

The aim is to get to know what's living and growing in your area. It would be useful to look up what you'd be likely to find in advance, so that you can identify what you see. It is also helpful to have interesting facts on hand about the behaviour and growth of the things you might see – once you have one interesting hook, it makes learning much easier.

5. Bird boxes

Buy or make bird boxes. If you don't have a garden, see if your local school, church, nature reserve or park would appreciate them.

6. Plant a tree

Trees not only take carbon out of the atmosphere and store it for many decades, they also support biodiversity. Trees in some areas can have as many as a thousand different species living on them! It would be useful to do some research about local tree species to find out what will do well in the area where you want to plant. As with the bird boxes, if you don't have a garden see if your local school, church, nature reserve or park would appreciate some trees being planted.

7. Learn about local natural history and ecosystems

Look for activities in your area where you can do this.

8. Campaign

If you don't have the facilities to recycle, take public transport or cycle in your area, **write to local politicians** asking to increase (or introduce) funding for these things in the local area.

Taking it Further

Websites:

A carbon footprint calculator and carbon offset scheme
www.climatestewards.net

Resources from a Christian conservation group
http://en.arocha.org/home

A Rocha's lifestyle challenge
www.livinglightly24-1.org.uk

Resources and articles
www.jri.org.uk

Articles and courses
www.ausable.org

The UK 'Ecocongregation' scheme
www.ecocongregation.org

Environment resources from the American Scientific Affiliation
www.asa3.org/aSa/topics/environment/index.html

Evangelical Environment Network (US)
www.creationcare.org

Articles to download:

John Houghton, 'Why Care for the Environment'
www.st-edmunds.cam.ac.uk/faraday/resources/Faraday%20Papers/Faraday%20Paper%205%20Houghton_EN.pdf

John Houghton, 'Global Warming, Climate Change and Sustainability'
www.jri.org.uk/brief/Briefing_14_3rd_edition.pdf

'Climate Change Controversies: A Simple Guide' from The Royal Society, 2007
http://royalsociety.org/page.asp?id=6229

Robert White, 'A Burning Issue: Christian Care for the Environment'
www.jubilee-centre.org/document.php?id=53

Books:

Hilary Marlow, *The Earth Is the Lord's: A Biblical Response to Environmental Issues* (Grove Books, 2008). Looking at a range of texts and themes in the Old and New Testaments, this study shows how the whole of the non-human created order is included in the biblical vision of God's restoration. It includes questions for reflection and points to resources for practical action.

Colin A. Russell, *Saving Planet Earth: A Christian Response* (Authentic, 2008). This is a very introductory level book, rich in facts about the environment, theological reflection on the Bible and practical suggestions. It addresses some questions which might be more specific to the evangelical wing of the church.

Dave Bookless, *Planetwise: Dare to Care for God's World* (IVP, 2008). This is an introductory level book setting out what the Bible says about why and how Christians should care for God's earth. It is full of practical illustrations and suggestions as well as biblical material. It also includes follow-up questions and resources.

Martin J. and Margot R. Hodson, *Cherishing the Earth: How to Care for God's Creation* (Monarch, 2008). This is a stimulating and inspiring Christian response to environmental issues from a scientist and a theologian. It includes chapters on the science of global warming and on the effect on the world's poor and challenges our attitudes and lifestyles.

Nick Spencer and Robert White, *Christianity, Climate Change and Sustainable Living* (SPCK, 2007; US edition in press). Spencer and White look at the science behind climate change and the biblical imperative behind Christian engagement with environmental issues. They diagnose modern cultural problems leading to climate change and include practical suggestions for ways to integrate care for creation at different levels of life.

Sheet 1: 'What on earth am I doing? A personal lifestyle audit'

(Adapted with permission from Ruth Valerio, author of *L is for Lifestyle: Christian Living that Doesn't Cost the Earth* [IVP, 2008].)

Being a Christian should challenge us to face the issues of our world around us and do something about them. These questions provide a measure for checking out your lifestyle and thinking with reference to the environment. Your answers and scores should be a stimulus for discussion and action – mark yourself as honestly as you can! Use the definitions below to clarify the questions. Please tick a box for each question.

I Buy:	I do it	I think about it	It doesn't cross my mind
Environmentally friendly washing powder / liquid			
Items with less packaging (whenever possible)			
Items with less transport miles (when aware)			
Recycled paper / envelopes / toilet paper and kitchen roll / paper towel			
I recycle:			
Newspapers / waste paper			
Glass			
Aluminium or steel cans and plastic			
Garden waste			
Kitchen waste			
Clothes / books			
I make a point of using:			
Local shops instead of out-of-town supermarkets			
Local farmer's markets and farm shops			
Public transport / car sharing			
A bike instead of a car			
A car with a small engine			
Energy-saving light bulbs			
Lights / electrical equipment and turn off when finished (not on stand-by)			
Produce which I have grown / made myself			
Gas and electricity from a green energy provider (where available)			
I support:			
Local conservation groups			
National environmental organizations			
Birds, by providing food in my garden and putting bells on any cats I own			
Local wildlife by gardening organically			
Add up your scores in their columns			
Each point is worth	2	1	0
Grand total	+	=	

Test of Faith – Session 2: An Accident in the Making? Creation, Evolution and Interpreting Genesis 79
www.testoffaith.com

SESSION 2

See page 56 of the **Study Guide**

Scores and Definitions

0–16	Being a Christian doesn't impact your lifestyle or thinking about these issues much. Choose an issue which interests you and discover how you can make a difference.
17–32	You're thinking about making a difference, but getting around to it remains a challenge. It's time to do those things you've been putting off!
32–48	Your lifestyle reflects that you've made changes. Challenge yourself to find out more and keep going!

Environmentally friendly means being sensitive to the need to reduce the use of natural resources, considering pollution and the amount of energy used by producing or using a product.

Transport miles refer to the mileage covered by an item from the producer of the raw ingredients to the shop floor. For example, a locally grown potato may travel to a washing centre and then to a distribution centre before it reaches your local superstore, however the local market will sell it dirty direct from the farm! More transport is used, and therefore more congestion and pollution are produced, by shopping at superstores.

Recycling is the idea of using materials again. If an item cannot be re-used in its present form, it can be broken down and the materials used again. This process uses far less energy and fewer natural resources than using raw materials each time.

Car sharing makes use of spare seats in cars when two or more people are travelling to the same destination at the same time.

Farmers markets are markets where local producers can sell their goods direct to the customer. In the UK they must come from within a 30-mile radius and the stall has to be staffed by the actual producer. The produce is not only fresher but often also contains few chemicals. Less packaging and transportation are required, which means there is less waste and fewer road journeys. Farmers markets also encourage people to try home-produced, regional specialities.

Bicycling is a far more environmentally friendly means of transportation than driving. For example, a bicycle can be pedalled for up to 1037 km on the energy equivalent of one litre of petrol (nearly 300 mpg). In addition, a regular adult cyclist on average exhibits the fitness levels of someone ten years younger.

Session 3: Is Anybody There?
Freedom to Choose

Planning

Aim

This session moves the discussion on to even more practical issues, exploring who we are as human beings made in the image of God. The discoveries of neuroscientists can – if we look only at the surface of some people's arguments – make us question the reality of our own experiences. But understanding these findings properly can help us to learn more about who we are.

The aim of Part 3 of the documentary is to help the viewer understand:

- Who am I in the light of scientific discovery about the brain?
- The importance of rejecting reductionism. We are not simply a product of our genes. We cannot simply be reduced to collections of neurons (brain cells). (Bonus Session 3b will tackle the concept of emergence.)
- We have the ability to make moral choices, and we need to think carefully about new technologies.

The discussion time should equip people (scientifically and biblically) to develop informed opinions on these scientific and ethical issues.

Note: Sessions 3 and 3b deal with some medical ethical issues which may be very sensitive or painful for some members of the group – particularly if beginning of life issues are brought up (IVF, abortion, testing for genetic disease, etc.). As discussion leader it's important to be sensitive to potential areas of hurt and to steer the discussion in such a way that people who are struggling with decisions in these areas don't feel embarrassed or condemned in any way.

Some suggestions for a 1 ½ – 2 hour session:

	Basic introduction A	Basic introduction B	In-depth	Big picture	A group with a lot of scientific knowledge
Introduction Option	3	1 or 2	3	1 or 2	3
DVD	✓	✓	✓	✓	✓
Ch. 1: The 'God Spot'		✓		✓	
Ch. 2: Whole Persons / Choices, Choices …				✓	
Ch. 3: An Ethical Toolkit	✓		✓		✓
Ch. 3: Using Your Ethical Toolkit: Cloning			✓		✓
Epilogue Option	2	1	any	3	any

Test of Faith – Session 3: Is Anybody There? Freedom to Choose 81
www.testoffaith.com

SESSION 3

To split into two shorter sessions *(40–60 minutes each)*

Ask the group to read the material relating to this session in the *Study Guide* beforehand.

First half-session:
- Introduction activity in pairs *(5 minutes)*
- DVD – watch and discuss for 5 minutes after each chapter
- Epilogue *(5 minutes)*

Second half-session:
- Quick recap by leader *(5 minutes)*
- Finish watching DVD if needed
- Discussion Topics – pick one or two that raised the most interest, or split into smaller groups to discuss different topics
- Epilogue *(5 minutes)*

Preparation for Participants *(optional)*:
Who am I?

The aim of this activity is to get people thinking about what makes an individual – genetic, environmental, relational and spiritual influences. If people are able to do this preparation, the discussion during the session will be more relevant to each person in the group. If you use this activity, then Introduction Option 1 or 2 would be most appropriate.

Ask two or three friends, family members or colleagues to think of two things about themselves (physical characteristic, talent, interest, like/dislike, etc.):

1. Something that they believe they inherited from a parent. (Although unless it's an obvious physical characteristic it's difficult to figure out whether it was learned from them or actually inherited – you'll just have to guess!)

2. Something that they think came from another source. (E.g., something learned from people around them, something in their physical or cultural environment, a spiritual experience, a new opportunity, or perhaps something they developed by themselves.)

or

Ask a relative or family friend what things they think that you inherited from parents and what things are unique to you, and perhaps sometimes surprising?

Introduction: What makes you you? *(10–15 minutes)*

The aim is to start thinking about ourselves as whole persons, mind and body, or about the factors that influence our ethical decisions.

Option 1:

Q: What different events and influences have made you the person that you are today?

Hints:
- *physical (I have a good ear for music, I'm short-sighted.)*
- *spiritual (My family were Christians.)*
- *relational (When I was sixteen it was a teacher who inspired me to take Biology seriously.)*
- *environmental (I was born in the UK.)*

Option 2:

Q: Can you think of one significant thing that has affected who you are as a person today?

Hints:
It may be difficult to say, but the question should get people thinking. Hopefully there will be a range of different answers. Examples:

- *A person*
- *An opportunity*
- *A spiritual experience*
- *An illness or physical characteristic*

Option 3:

Q: People use all sorts of criteria for making ethical decisions, for example in medical situations – and sometimes quite unconsciously. How many can you think of?

Hints:
Specifically Christian sources:[iii]

- *The Bible*
- *Church teaching*
- *Conscience / conviction by the Holy Spirit*
- *The wisdom and informed opinions of others*

Secular:

- *'Gut feelings', an emotional decision – 'yuk' or 'wow'*
- *Reason / logic*
- *Conscience / guilt*
- *Consensus – following the crowd, often hugely affected by media treatment of the issue*
- *Utilitarian – consequences, the best outcome*
- *Relativism – 'that's true for you' … ethics is a private matter*
- *Authority*

Watch *Test of Faith* Part 3: Is Anybody There? *(45–60 minutes)*

Use the chapter menu to watch Part 3 of the documentary a chapter at a time. Pause the DVD at the end of each chapter using the cues below (press pause after you hear the cue).

Chapter 1 – Alasdair Coles: '…there may well be more to it that isn't accommodated by the scientific method.' [Time code: 5 min. 20]
Chapter 2 – John Polkinghorne: '…not as collections of quarks and gluons or whatever it might be.' [Time code: 12 min. 51]
Chapter 3 – John Polkinghorne: '…it's not the whole story about us, we are more than computers made of meat, or something like that.' [Time code: 22 min. 11]

After each chapter take a few minutes (depending on the size of your group) to help people process what they have just seen. For general discussion use an open question such as:

- What was new or most interesting for you?
- What did you find most surprising or challenging?
- What do you think the main messages were?
- What do you think? Do you agree?

Or you could use the Short Questions below.

Short Questions:

Chapter 1

Q: **Where does the debate about neuroscience and faith come from? Why is there any controversy?**

A: Some people claim that neuroscience has shown that: a) what we do and who we are is determined purely by our biological makeup; and b) spiritual experiences are just a by-product of the normal workings of the brain – they have no spiritual meaning at all.

Q: **If spiritual experiences are accompanied by activity in certain parts of the brain, does that mean that spiritual experience is meaningless, and God is not involved?**

A: No. Both David Wilkinson and Alasdair Coles say that knowing that brain activity happens doesn't rule out a higher, spiritual meaning. As we discussed in Session 1, there are questions that science cannot answer.

Chapter 2

Q: **What are the two reasons why someone *can't* say that what we do is determined entirely by our brains?**

A1: Our environment also shapes us.

A2: You can't predict our complicated behaviours just by looking at our brains – a unique mind 'emerges' from the parts that make our bodies.

Chapter 3

Q: **If it was ever possible to clone someone, would a clone be an exact copy of the person who was cloned?**

A: No, because our genes alone do not determine our identity. Other factors, such as the environment we live in and our relationships with God and others, are also important.

Q: **These scientists say that human beings have three characteristics that show we are not just 'computers made of meat'. What are they?**

A: Our creative abilities, moral reasoning, and our ability to make choices. Even if science could ever explain the mechanism of how these occur, it could not explain why we still believe that they are meaningful.

Chapter 4

Q: **What two ways of discovering truth does Francis Collins mention?**

A: The book of the Bible and the book of nature.

Q: **Francis Collins says that we mustn't be afraid to investigate the world, but he does follow the 'two books' idea with a warning. About what do we need to be careful?**

A: You need to carefully consider which tool you're using to answer which type of question. (An example of this is the 'God spot' idea in the Discussion Topic for Chapter 1. People who propose a 'God spot' are trying to use scientific tools to answer a spiritual question.)

Glossary	
altruism	Unselfish concern for others (which may involve self-sacrificial acts).
cell	The units that make up a living thing. Animal cells consist of a membrane enclosing whatever parts that particular type of cell needs to do its job. A fat cell contains fat, a bone cell contains a hard substance, a red blood cell contains a substance that carries oxygen around the body, and the long spindly nerve cells are able to pass electrical signals along their length.
emergence	The idea that complex structures have properties that you couldn't predict if you looked at their individual parts.
neurons	The 'nerve cells' that carry messages in the nervous system and the brain.
neuroscience	The study of the brain and nervous system.
reductionist	Someone who thinks that you can explain everything by reducing it to its most basic physical properties.

Discussion Topics *(25–30 minutes)*

The topics below relate to each of the four DVD chapters. Pick one or two to discuss. You may want to watch the relevant chapter again as a refresher, especially if you are spreading the course over more than one session.

(?) Chapter 1: The 'God Spot'　　　　　　　　　　　　　*Level: Easy*

Dr Alasdair Coles says that some neuroscientists [*not* including himself] believe that spiritual experiences are just a side effect of the brain's normal function. [Time code: 3 min. 13]

> **Q:** **The scientists interviewed and many others (of many faiths and none) have rejected the idea of a 'God spot' in our brains. Do you think they're right? Use the two quotes below to help you:**
>
> " [There's] a place in the brain for everything. You know there's a Jennifer Aniston spot and there's a hamburger spot in my brain and in yours. Anything you know anything about, **anything you have any bunch of beliefs about, there's got to be something in your brain that's holding those.**
>
> Professor Daniel Dennett, philosopher[iv]
>
> " If someone wanted to come along and link me up to electrodes while I was praying or while I was in worship and found that my brain patterns were slightly different, then that wouldn't be a great surprise to me. I think spiritual experience is real and therefore there should be a way of looking at that in terms of the physicality of the brain. **But just to look at those brain patterns and to say that that is all that spiritual experience is seems to me to be mistaken.**
>
> Dr David Wilkinson [Time code: 3 min. 56]

(?) Chapter 2: Whole Persons　　　　　　　　　　　　*Level: Intermediate*

The aim of this section is to think about ourselves as whole beings – body, mind and spirit or soul. Because we are more than machines, we do have the ability to make meaningful choices. (Bonus Session 3b will deal with the concept of emergence.)

Note: *What we are saying about the soul in this section is not necessarily that we do not have immaterial souls, but that our bodies are also important because: a) there is obviously an interaction between what we think or experience and what happens in our brains; and b) God created us with physical bodies in the first place. Recognizing the importance of our bodies equips us to have a meaningful discussion about advances in scientific knowledge about the brain, and especially where they concern spirituality.*

Dr Alasdair Coles says that we are not simply machines, and neither are we disembodied souls with no real connection to our physical bodies. A person's body, mind and soul are interdependent. [Time code: 23 min. 47]

With this in mind, read Mark 12:28–30.

SESSION 3

Test of Faith – Session 3: Is Anybody There? Freedom to Choose　85
www.testoffaith.com

Q1: How could you obey this command?

Hint:

 • *Think about things that involve each of the following: heart, soul, mind, strength.*

Note: *This is a good point to end on if you're short of time – and move on to worship.*

Read the account of Jesus' resurrection appearance in Luke 24: 36–44 and his promise that we will be resurrected in John 5:28–29.

Our physical bodies are clearly important to God – not just the part of us that may be purely spiritual. There is somehow continuity between our physical bodies here and now and our resurrected bodies.

Q2: What ideas have you heard or read about the body and spirit or soul? How do those ideas compare to the account in the passages you have just read?

Hint:

 • *The continuity between our physical bodies now and our resurrected bodies is part of Christian orthodoxy, but it is sometimes overlooked. We know that our physical bodies do not survive in their current form, and we can see them failing as we age or become sick, so we often think about the spirit surviving and leaving the body behind – thereby forgetting about the interdependence of our body, mind and spirit. The mysteries of the time between death and resurrection, or of the form of the resurrected body when we know that the physical body decays, should not deter us from recognizing this interdependence. See the 'Taking it Further' section for resources to investigate this topic further.*

Choices, choices ...

Professor Bill Newsome says that although there are obviously some things that we can't do (not all of us can play golf like Tiger Woods, for example), we do have the ability to make meaningful choices. [Time code: 20 min. 45`]

Read Joshua 24:14–15, keeping in mind this idea of making choices.

Q3: What does this passage say about our ability to choose?

Hint:

 • *Throughout the Bible people are asked to choose and are held responsible for their choices. This is a good working definition of that much-discussed concept of free will.*

Q4: *(If it's at all necessary to reinforce this point.)* **Think of a conscious choice that you made that changed the course of your life.**

(?) ## Chapter 3: An Ethical Toolkit   *Level: Intermediate*

Because Chapter 4 is a conclusion, and more relevant to the Epilogue, there are two Discussion Topics for Chapter 3.

This section will challenge people to think about how we use our ability to make moral choices – and to apply that to the cloning technology in Chapter 3 of the DVD. The 'ethical toolkit' is the most important part of this section because it equips people to think about new ethical issues for themselves.

To tackle ethical issues from a Christian perspective you first need to construct a moral framework, or 'ethical toolkit', from biblical principles.

Q: What moral principles can you draw from the following Bible passages?

You could split into pairs to read and discuss these and report back to the whole group.

Genesis 1:26–27

- We are made in the 'image of God'. This supports the value and dignity of every human life and has ethical consequences (Genesis 9:6; James 3:9–10).

Galatians 3:26–29; Romans 12:4–8

- Each individual is important, regardless of their abilities and whether these are genetically based or otherwise.

Mark 12:31; Philippians 2:3–4

- Love your neighbour as yourself, look to the interests of others.

Deuteronomy 10:18

- It's necessary to protect and care for the vulnerable.

Matthew 25:31–46

- Care for the suffering.

Psalms 127:3–5

- Children are gifts from God.

(?) Using Your Ethical Toolkit: Cloning[v]   *Level: Intermediate*

Cloning (often called 'reproductive cloning') is making a genetic copy of a person – the process would be like taking a cell from someone's body and using it as a seed to grow a new person.

Q1: Some babies born naturally are genetic clones of each other – identical twins! Thinking about any identical twins that you have met, what can you tell about how much our genes determine our different characteristics?

Hint:

- Identical twins come from the same fertilized egg, but we know that they are unique individuals – therefore other influences have a significant effect on a person during development (relational, environmental, cultural, etc.).

Q2: Why do you think someone might want to artificially 'clone' a person?

Hints:

- Infertility (although the child would only be the child of one parent)
- To replace a child or person who died
- Duplication of talented individuals
- To allow a homosexual couple to have a child (again, the child would only be the child of one parent)
- Curiosity
- A source of compatible tissue for transplants (as in the movie The Island)
- The cult called the Raelian Movement believes that cloning will bring immortality

SESSION 3

Test of Faith – Session 3: Is Anybody There? Freedom to Choose 87
www.testoffaith.com

Read the case study on page 91 and answer the following questions, bearing in mind your 'ethical toolkit'.

Q3: Can you anticipate some of the consequences of cloning this child? How might it affect the resulting clone, their family, and the rest of society?

Hints:

- *The child will struggle with huge expectations to be just like the deceased child.*
- *The parents will probably be disappointed that the clone is not like the original child.*
- *The financial cost will be enormous.*

Q4: Can you anticipate some of the consequences of people cloning themselves and bringing these clones up as their own children? On the children? The parents? Society?

Hints:

- *One risk is making people commodities that you can buy.*
- *The clones will see their older selves and might feel a sense of fatalism, especially if they see the diseases from which the older versions of themselves suffer. Being exact copies, they will wonder if they will suffer from the same things.*
- *Who is the clone's parent? If an adult clones him or herself, the child's 'biological parents' are actually its grandparents.*
- *It is another way for children to be born outside of a family.*

The procedure of cloning poses huge medical risks:

- A very high miscarriage rate.
- The cell from the cloned person is 'old', and the new child made from that cell will inherit that age (including cancer risks), rather than having their 'clock' re-set by the process of egg formation. This is a process that biologists don't understand fully, so it is difficult to predict the results or reduce the risk.
- In the process of making eggs and sperm, certain genes are switched on and off. A clone whose 'parent' is a fully developed cell may not inherit the correct switching required for normal development.

Q5: Think back to the motivations for cloning a child discussed in Q2. Do you think any of these would justify taking the risk of cloning a child?

To help your discussion:

- *Most of the motivations (apart from creating organs for transplant, which is an extreme example of commodification of humans) are not to save lives, so most bioethicists argue that cloning is not worth the risk.*

Epilogue *(10–15 minutes)*

Option 1:

Read Psalm 139. Use this to begin a prayer time focusing on praising God for who he has made us to be.

Option 2:

Think of ethical issues that are in the news at the moment and pray for the people involved in them. Is there anything that members of the group could do to get involved? (E.g., writing to Members of Parliament [UK] or members of Congress [US], or responding to a government consultation.)

If you have non-believers in your group you could talk about current issues. What has challenged you? How you can get involved? Try to do something before the next session.

Option 3:

Epilogue Option 1 from Session 1b (Supporting Christians in Science) would also be appropriate.

Option 4:

If you haven't already used it, use Q1 from the 'Whole Persons' Discussion Topic as an epilogue. Spend time individually writing answers down and then pray as a group, or in small groups, through the different ways we can serve God as whole people.

Option 5:

Some of this session may have hit very close to home for certain members of the group – if it's appropriate, pray through these things.

Option 6:

If you are doing Sessions 1, 2 and 3 only, this will be your last session. If you would like to do a recap or debrief activity, see the Epilogue Options for Bonus Session 3b.

Option 7:

If you would like to sing, you could use one of the songs or hymns on the list in Appendix 3 on page 113.

Further Activity

If you want to do a practical activity – either as a group or individually – you could pick one of the groups listed in the links section below and find a way to get involved or take part in an event or activity that they have organized.

Test of Faith – Session 3: Is Anybody There? Freedom to Choose 89
www.testoffaith.com

SESSION 3

Taking it Further

Websites and articles to download:

John Bryant, 'Don't My Genes Determine My Behaviour?'
www.eauk.org/resources/idea/bigquestion/archive/2005/bq9.cfm

Denis Alexander, 'Cloning Humans – Distorting the Image of God?'
www.jubilee-centre.org/document.php?id=32&topicID=0

Ethics resources from the American Scientific Affiliation
www.asa3.org/ASA/topics/ethics/default.html

The Christian Medical Fellowship (UK)
www.cmf.org.uk

BioCentre (formerly The Centre for Bioethics and Public Policy) (UK)
www.bioethics.ac.uk

Center for Bioethics and Human Dignity (USA)
www.cbhd.org

Books:

John Bryant and John Searle, *Life in Our Hands: A Christian Perspective on Genetics and Cloning* (IVP, 2004). With an eye to the practical application of new technologies, Bryant and Searle lay out the ethical dilemmas facing biological scientists and explore the theological implications. They outline the ethical position that they have reached on each issue, but not before showing the various positions that Christians take and emphasizing how difficult it can be to decide in matters that affect life and death.

Tony Watkins (ed.), *Playing God: Talking about Ethics in Medicine and Technology* (Authentic/Damaris Publications, 2006). *Playing God* tackles ethical issues in a different way, following the Damaris route of using films and books – including a television medical drama, Jodie Picoult's *My Sister's Keeper*, the writings of Isaac Asimov, Margaret Atwood's *Oryx and Crake*, and the ethics of Peter Singer – to discuss the topics. This is an easy but thought-provoking read and could be the basis for a group study.

Pete Moore, *Babel's Shadow: Genetic Technologies in a Fracturing Society* (Lion, 2000). Written by a biologist who is an experienced science writer and ethics lecturer, this book covers the broad issues involved in decisions concerning genetics and its medical applications. Although written before the completion of the Human Genome Project, the principles here still apply and this book is an excellent and very readable introduction to the topic.

John Wyatt, *Matters of Life and Death: Today's Healthcare Dilemmas in the Light of Christian Faith* (IVP, 1998). In writing this book John Wyatt draws on his experience as Professor of Neonatal Paediatrics and Consultant Neonatal Paediatrician at University College London. This is a very thorough introduction to the issues and draws on a lot of biblical material. It covers reproductive technology, foetal screening, genetics, abortion, neonatal care and euthanasia.

Case Study[vi]

The fog on the M4 was exceptionally dense as the Robinson family drove towards London on November 20th, 2011. Their only child Susan, aged four, was playing happily with her dolls on the back seat. After years of unsuccessfully trying for a baby the Robinsons had eventually decided to use *in vitro* fertilization to have Susan, so she was especially cherished. Her long eyelashes and dimples were the spitting image of her mum, whereas even at that young age her long limbs held great promise of future athletic prowess, or so her proud father liked to think.

Suddenly a pile-up loomed out of the fog in front of them. Mr Robinson slammed on the brakes. His quick responses prevented their car diving into the mangled heap of wrecked cars ahead, but unfortunately the lorry driver behind was not so alert, sliding into their rear with a sickening thud. Seconds later the shocked parents found themselves clutching Susan's lifeless form as they huddled on the embankment, waiting for help to arrive.

Minutes later, after a short but fevered discussion, Mrs Robinson called CLON777 on her mobile and as the fog began to clear a helicopter landed in a nearby field, CLONE-AID emblazoned across its fuselage. A white-coated medical technician leapt from the helicopter and was soon taking tiny skin samples from Susan's limp body. Minutes later the samples were being stimulated in a nearby CLONE-AID laboratory to establish cell cultures.

Several months went by whilst the Robinsons grieved for little Susan, but finally they could contain themselves no longer. They wanted a replacement Susan and they wanted her now. Fortunately Mrs Robinson already had viable eggs frozen down as a result of her cycle of *in vitro* fertilization. The great day came. In the CLONE-AID laboratory, with its picture of Dolly the sheep proudly displayed on the wall, the process of 'nucleus transfer' began. A nucleus was removed from one of Susan's cultured skin cells. This single nucleus contained the cell's DNA with its genetic instructions to build a new Susan. Carefully the nucleus was placed in a small dish with one of Mrs Robinson's eggs from which the nucleus had been removed. A small electric current was zapped through the cell suspension and the nucleus fused with the egg cell to produce a tiny embryo. This procedure was repeated multiple times to generate several embryos that were carefully screened over the next few days to check for any abnormalities before one of them was implanted in Mrs Robinson. Nine months later the Robinsons held in their arms a pink and gorgeous looking 'replacement Susan', complete with dimples, prominent eyelashes and long limbs.

Cloning explained:[vii]

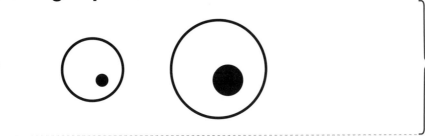

1 An adult cell (left) and egg cell (right). The DNA of both cells is contained in a structure called the nucleus, represented by the solid black circles. The adult cell contains two sets of DNA; the unfertilized egg contains one.

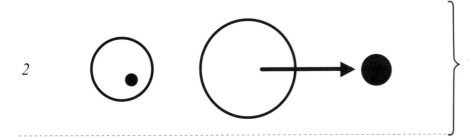

2 The nucleus is removed from the egg cell

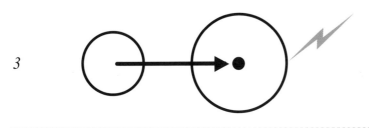

3 The egg cell nucleus is replaced with a nucleus from the adult cell. The new cell-nucleus combination is stimulated to divide (as a normally fertilized egg would), often by a very brief electric shock. If an embryo is formed it is placed in the womb in order to establish a pregnancy. It will be a genetic copy of the adult from which the nucleus (containing the DNA) was taken.

SESSION 3

Bonus Session 3b: Is Anybody There?
Thinking about Human Identity

Planning

Aim

The aim of this session is to examine in more depth the issues that the DVD and Session 3 raised. The main questions for Session 3b are: What does it mean to be made in the image of God? And how, therefore, do we view genetic testing and enhancement? This session also explores emergence.

Note: *Once again, this session deals with some medical ethical issues which may be very sensitive or painful for some members of the group – particularly if beginning of life issues are brought up (IVF, abortion, testing for genetic disease etc.). As discussion leader it's important to be sensitive to potential areas of hurt and to steer the discussion in such a way that people who are struggling with decisions in these areas don't feel embarrassed or condemned in any way.*

Equipment needed

You will need to use the DVD bonus interviews for this session. See the 'bonus features' section of the DVD for details.

Some suggestions for a 1 ½ – 2 hour session:

	Basic introduction	In depth, including the beginning of life	In depth, no beginning of life	For a group with a lot of scientific knowledge
Introduction Option	1 or 3	2	1	1 or 2
The Image of God	✓	✓	✓	✓
The Beginning of Life	✓	✓		
Genetic Testing	Either this	Either this		✓
Enhancement	or this	or this	✓	✓
Emergence		✓	✓	✓
Epilogue Option	any	any	any	any

To split into two shorter sessions *(40–60 minutes each)*

Ask the group to read the material relating to this session in the *Study Guide* beforehand.

First half-session:
- Introduction activity in pairs *(5–10 minutes)*
- Discussion Topics – pick one or two
- Epilogue *(5–10 minutes)*

Second half-session:
- Quick recap by leader *(5 minutes)*
- Discussion Topics – pick one or two more
- Epilogue *(5–10 minutes)*

Preparation for Participants *(optional):*
Ethics

Read one of the articles from the 'Taking it Further' section for this session.

or (more introductory)

Explore one of the websites recommended in the 'Taking it Further' section for Session 3, looking for information on the 'Image of God'.

Introduction *(10–15 minutes)*

Option 1:

Q: What it is about you that makes you human?

We will explore this in more detail in discussion topic 1.

For a large group, discuss in pairs or small groups and report back the characteristics that you think are most important.

Option 2:

If you used the Discussion Topic 'An Ethical Toolkit' in Session 3, has laying out that framework had any impact on your own decision making since then? How much of it can you remember?

Option 3:

Q: Some things have a property that cannot be predicted by looking at their individual parts. For example, words have a meaning that could not be predicted from looking at a jumbled up list of letters. Can you think of any other examples?

This is to introduce the concept of emergence.

Discussion Topics *(60–90 minutes)*

Pick two or three of these to discuss. The video clips are on the 'bonus' menu of the DVD.

(?) The Image of God   *Level: Intermediate*

The aim of this section is to try to define what we mean by the phrase 'made in the image of God', and what that means for our lives.

Read Genesis 1:26–28 and Genesis 2:15–17.

Q1: What do you think the phrase 'made in the image of God' means? What is it about us that is different from other living creatures?

Hint:
- *God gave us the responsibility to 'rule' over the earth, and also the gift of a personal relationship with God.*

Q2: How would you define human uniqueness in a secular context? Is it possible?

This is partly to show how different a definition would be in this context, and also how difficult it is to define human uniqueness without reference to anything spiritual.

Watch the bonus interview: 3.1 David Wilkinson *(2 min. 15 sec.)*

Glossary	
The Near East	A term archaeologists and historians use for the Middle East.

Q3: **Some of the definitions of 'the image of God' or human uniqueness that you came up with above might exclude some people. How is the description David Wilkinson gives more inclusive?**

Hints:

- *Definitions based on the ability to reason, imagine or do specific tasks exclude infants and people who don't have those abilities. But if our uniqueness is based on our relationship with God, as well as on our responsibility as 'stewards', then that includes everyone.*

Read Genesis 9:5–6 and James 3:7–10.

Q4: **What are the consequences of being made in the image of God? How does that affect you?**

Hint:

- *We take care of people out of respect for God's image in them.*

The Beginning of Life

Level: Intermediate

 Watch the bonus interview: 3.2 John Bryant *(45 sec.)*

Read the Briefing Sheet: When Does Human Life Begin?

These are the most commonly held views on the status of embryos and the arguments that are used to support them.

- *What we are talking about is this: to what do we ascribe human personhood?*
- *Twinning: identical twins are formed when a single embryo divides into two. This can happen during the first two weeks of pregnancy.*

Q: **What do you think of the different views laid out here?**

Counter-arguments (in favour of life beginning at fertilization):

- *There is a high risk of embryo loss at this stage, but just because life is shorter doesn't make it less important. Just because something has a high risk of dying doesn't mean it isn't valuable, or human.*
- *Although at this stage you cannot tell the difference between what will become placenta and what will become the embryo, this means that before implantation it is more than a human, not less.*
- *This is simply picking an aspect of a human (e.g., nervous system or intelligence) and defining them by it. People used to say it was when the heart began beating, now it's the nervous system.*
- *There is a difference between saying that we don't know whether one or two persons will result from fertilization (in the case of twinning) and saying that there are no persons at all present.*

Counter-arguments (in favour of life beginning later than fertilization):

- *The passage referring to the incarnation of Jesus, and those in Isaiah and Jeremiah, are talking about pregnancy and not fertilization – and in some cases they are named before fertilization occurs.*
- *Personal history only applies to those who survive.*
- *Fertilization itself is not a one off, single event but a gradual process.*
- *Twinning may occur until implantation, so until this occurs there isn't 'one' individual present to relate to God.*

Counter-argument (against life beginning with nervous system development):

- *Although a very early nervous system is present at 14 days, sensation is not possible until much later.*

Note: *Most people who argue for human life beginning at the later stages would still argue that early embryos are not simply disposable – they are human material and work in this area must be strictly regulated.*

Genetic Testing

Level: Intermediate

▶ Watch the bonus interview: **3.3 Denis Alexander** *(1 min. 15 sec.)*

Q1: What might be the arguments for and against testing for genetic diseases, and the possible destruction of affected embryos (this could happen by testing IVF embryos and deciding which ones to use)?

Hints:

- *You could go back to the 'ethical toolkit' question in Session 3 for ideas.*
- *In thinking it through we need to ask which of these reasons are truly justifiable.*

Arguments for:

- *An act of compassion for the individual who would die early from the disease.*
- *An act of compassion for the parents – will they cope?*

Arguments against:

- *It involves destruction of vulnerable human embryos.*
- *It is a form of 'eugenics' – discrimination against certain genetic types.*
- *Increasing 'commodification' of human embryos – they are like things that we select or dispose of as we wish.*
- *Increasing intolerance of and discrimination against disability in society.*
- *Certain diseases are not sufficiently serious to affect the life of the individual or the parents enough to justify destruction of the embryo.*
- *No disease is serious enough to justify destruction of embryos. Just because life is shorter or more painful doesn't make it less important.*

Q2: Who else do you think is affected by genetic testing, in addition to the embryo?

Hints:

- *Parents, couples or individuals who have to make decisions about genetic testing, have been through unsuccessful pregnancies or IVF, or have decided not to have children because of an inherited disease in the family.*
- *Individuals who are affected by genetic disease.*
- *Doctors and healthcare workers, including Christians who feel called to work in these areas.*
- *Families and friends of the above people.*

 # Enhancement

Level: Intermediate

▶ Watch the bonus interview: **3.4 John Bryant, Francis Collins and John Polkinghorne** *(5 min.)*

Glossary	
cognitive ability	The ability to think and experience things.
transhumanism	The idea of enhancing human abilities with technology in extreme ways.
preimplantation genetic diagnosis	DNA testing of IVF embryos.

Note: some of the treatments discussed in this section are not available now, but might be in the future.

SESSION 3

See pages 69-70 of the **Study Guide**

Examples of some enhancement technologies:

1. Genetic modification, or GM (e.g., 'gene doping' in athletes) *(a speculation for the future)*:
   - to cause an effect in an individual
   - or to change the genes in their eggs or sperm so that the future generation is affected.

2. Prosthetics or implants (e.g., an artificial leg, brain implant, living tissue implant) *(many present realities)*

3. Chemicals or drugs (e.g., to enhance memory) *(present realities or will be with us soon)*

Q1: Look at the list of potential treatments below and put them on the spectrum, deciding where they should be on the line from healing to enhancement.

You could do this as a group or individually.
One approach is to think of healing as restoring to what's normal for most of the population.

1. Vaccination
2. Caffeine tablets
3. A memory implant (in a normal functioning person)
4. A third arm
5. GM to treat muscular dystrophy[vi]
6. Drugs to enhance concentration
7. GM to make someone taller[vii]
8. Glasses

Healing   Unacceptable enhancement

Q2: What does enhancement focus on? How might that affect the enhanced individual and his or her relationship with the rest of society?

Hints:
- *Enhancement focuses on the abilities of an individual, or on giving them new abilities.*

Relationships affected:
- *There will be expectations on that person to perform.*
- *Justice: is this enhancement available to all, or does it cause a wider rift between rich and poor?*
- *Enhancement increases differences between people, which could lead to conflict (e.g., jealousy or social injustice causing anger and conflict).*
- *In practice it is already being used in warfare (e.g., alertness drugs for pilots).*

Read Luke 4:18–19; 17:11–14.

Q3: What different effects does Christian healing have on society?

Hints:
- *Christian healing is to do with wider justice and relationships – in addition to one individual's quality of life.*
- *It takes into account poverty and oppression as well as the social implications of treatments (e.g., the social reintegration of the lepers).*

Q4: Do your answers to Q2 and Q3 change the way you would approach Q1?

Emergence

 Watch the bonus interview: 3.5 Bill Newsome *(1 min.)*

Q1: Can you think of any emergent properties in daily life?

Think back to Introduction Option 3 if you used it.

To help your discussion:

- **Emergent system** = a collection of things that, when arranged in a certain way, has different properties to the raw materials. For example, books: words are complex systems of letters, and books are complex systems of words. A word is more than the individual letters themselves, and a book is more than a 'system of words'.

- **Emergent property** = a characteristic or behaviour of the whole system. For example, a property of a word might be a definition or meaning.
A property of a book might be the specific story told.

 Watch the bonus interview: 3.6 Bill Newsome *(2 min.)*

Emergence can mean two things:

1. That the whole has a different, or higher, property than its parts. These properties can be defined scientifically, and this sort of emergence is not at all controversial (e.g., a table compared to a piece of wood – this is 'epistemological emergence').

2. That 'emergent phenomena' have real significance in the world. For most people this is not an important question for a table, but an important question for us is: 'Does human emotion have more meaning than the firing of neurons?' This type of emergence is impossible to prove scientifically. (This is 'ontological emergence').

Q2: What do someone else's emotions mean from these two points of view?

Hints:
My idea that someone is happy:

1. *Is an idea or construct that I have to help me to understand and predict their behaviour;*

2. *Is an understanding that is true of what they are experiencing.*

Q3: What are the implications of these two views for our ability to make choices? Which do you think makes the most sense?

Hints:

1. *If mind emerges from the brain in the first sense of emergence and does not 'exist', it is just a construct which we use because it is convenient, and we cannot really assign significance to it. In other words, we cannot accept that it has a causal power and so 'I', as a person, do not have any freedom or the ability to choose. Rather, I am completely determined by the physical processes of my brain.*

2. *If mind does 'exist', then I can have some degree of freedom and can have an influence on the processes of my brain.*

 Watch the bonus interview: 3.7 Bill Newsome *(1 min. 30 sec.)*

SESSION 3

Epilogue *(10–15 minutes)*

Use this time to wrap up, reflect and 'debrief' now that you have completed the course.

Option 1:

Think back over the course that you have just completed.

- What was the most important lesson that you learned?
- Will anything in the course change the way that you act?
- What idea will you pass on?
- Is there anything you want to look into in more depth?

Write down answers individually or talk about them in pairs or small groups.

You could spend some time praying about these things.

Option 2:

Think of things that you have learned in the course about the created world. Spend some time praising God for them.

Option 3:

What are the most important issues that have been raised in the course that affect the wider world? Spend some time praying for them.

What about ethical issues, the environment, or Christians working in science? (For this you could use Epilogue Option 1 from Bonus Session 1b.)

Option 4:

Look at the diagram of views on relating science and faith in Session 1, in the Discussion Topic 'How Do You View Science and Faith?' (page 24). What do you think now? Have your views changed or been clarified at all?

Option 5:

Use one of the Epilogue Options from Session 3.

Option 6:

If you would like to sing, you could use one of the songs or hymns on the list in Appendix 3 on page 113.

Taking it Further

See also the list from Session 3.

Articles to download:

Michael Poole, 'Reductionism: Help or Hindrance in Science and Religion?'
www.st-edmunds.cam.ac.uk/faraday/resources/Faraday%20Papers/Faraday%20Paper%206%20Poole_EN.pdf

John Bryant, 'Ethical Issues in Genetic Modification'
www.st-edmunds.cam.ac.uk/faraday/resources/Faraday%20Papers/Faraday%20Paper%207%20Bryant_EN.pdf

Books:

Pete Moore, *Enhancing Me: The Hope and Hype of Enhancement* (Wiley, 2008). While this was not written with the intention of giving specifically Christian teaching, it is a very readable and informative look at the latest enhancement technologies. It clearly separates the possible from the currently impossible and is in full colour with lots of pictures.

Appendix 1: Documentary Summary

Part 1: Beyond Reason?

Today, atheist critics of religion argue that science and faith are in conflict and that science eliminates the need for a Creator. Contemporary believing scientists argue otherwise. For them, science studies material processes but cannot and does not deal with ultimate questions of meaning and value. In recent decades, historians have also shown that science emerged from solid theological foundations in Christian Europe, suggesting that the idea of warfare between science and religion is relatively recent. Scientist-believers in the field of cosmology argue that the Big Bang says nothing about the existence or non-existence of God, while the laws of physics actually indicate we live in a wildly improbable universe. Although some atheist scientists claim a multiverse – or infinite number of universes – would explain our statistically unlikely universe, believing scientists see no threat in a multiverse. For them, God remains Creator, whether of one universe or many. Moreover, they maintain that God can hardly be threatened by any human knowledge, and that believers should embrace an intellectually questing spirit rather than pushing God into science's current gaps. However, the scientists spoken to here come from the realm of physics with its love of mathematical order and beauty. It has often appeared a very different picture in the realm of biology, with Charles Darwin's theory of evolution.

Part 2: An Accident in the Making?

Some evolutionary biologists maintain our world is one without design or purpose, one engineered by evolution rather than created by God. Believing scientists contest this claim. Two positions critical of evolution as an explanation for human life are Young Earth Creationism and Intelligent Design. Young Earth Creationists regard evolution as incompatible with faith. But evolution is actually compatible with many different metaphysical views, including faith ones. It is also backed up by robust genetic research. For the Human Genome Project's former director, and other believing scientists, it's natural to view evolution as God's mechanism for creating biological diversity – a position known as 'theistic evolution'. However, such scientist-believers still have to wrestle with questions of how pain, disease and death in evolution are compatible with a loving God. Evolution remains a complex, paradoxical process for them, with new life constantly emerging in the shadow of natural wastage and death. These scientists also point out that evolution provides no recipe for moral life. Indeed, they maintain that debates about evolution are secondary, at a time of unprecedented global warming, to the urgent Biblical command to care for creation. For them, science and faith must unite in helping finding solutions to this urgent problem. But there remains a further challenge to faith from science, and that's in the fields of genetics and neuroscience. Here, concepts of human free will and responsibility are being challenged as never before.

Part 3: Is Anybody There?

The Bible asserts that human beings are made in the image of God. But modern neuroscience and genetics claim that we run on rails laid down by our biology. Some atheist scientists say that brain imaging shows we are totally driven by our neurons and genes – even that spiritual experience is an illusion beginning and ending in our heads. However, scientist-believers disagree, arguing that there will always be neural correlates to any behaviour. Attempts to reduce human beings to sophisticated machines, they say, fail to account for our rich complexity. Moreover, contemporary theories of 'emergence' suggest that the brain is more than the sum of its parts. Instead, it is suggested that complex higher-level phenomena – such as 'mind' – emerge over a long evolutionary process. For these believing scientists, it is wrong to think that we are no more than our biological makeup. For them, human identity also depends on other key factors, including our relationship with others and our environment, and our own actions. Even a genetic clone would be far more than the sum of his or her DNA. Moreover, although genetics rightly points to our affinities with certain animals, humans are also distinguished by unique attributes like consciousness, creativity and moral awareness. For scientist-believers, in conclusion, human beings remain made in the image of God. The idea of science and religion in conflict is misguided. Both domains stem from our age-old desire to investigate and explore. And, for the believer, science can lead to increased wonder at God.

Appendix 2: Briefing Sheets
Briefing Sheet Session 1: Beyond Reason?

CHAPTER 1

The question we are faced with in society today is: **HAS SCIENCE DONE AWAY WITH FAITH?**

But many Christians who are also scientists have no problem reconciling their science and their faith.

The first scientists in the Western world were actually Christians.

The conflict we hear about in the media was mainly stirred up by Victorian scientists who wanted to get rid of the clergy who were involved in science.

One way of making sense of the difference between science and religion is to think of a boiling kettle.

How is it boiling? Because the element is heating the water.

Why is it boiling? Because I want some tea.

In the same way, science asks **'how?'** and religion asks **'why?'**

CHAPTER 2

These scientists believe that God created the universe. The **'how'** is answered by science - they see evidence that the universe started with a **'Big Bang'**.

We can make sense of the world using science and mathematics.

E.g. It was even possible to predict something as strange as antimatter using mathematics – several years before there was any physical proof for it.

But **why** is it like that? Is it because the universe was created by an intelligent being?

GOD OF THE GAPS

There is a lot about the universe that is still unexplained.

Are the unexplained parts proof for God? No, because scientists might find an explanation for these things in the future.

If we say these gaps are evidence for God, then if the evidence disappears, where is God?

It's far better to look at the whole picture and say, 'What an amazing creator!'

CHAPTER 4

DO WE LIVE IN A MULTIVERSE?

Some scientists explain the existence of life on earth by saying there are many universes, so it's not surprising that one has turned out like ours.

But there is no evidence at all for these other universes. Neither will it mean, if they do exist, that they are outside God's creation.

Science can only answer certain questions – it doesn't tell you anything about the meaning of life.

Faith isn't threatened by science. Why should we worry about finding out more about the world God created? In fact, the more we find out, the more we can be amazed by what God has made.

CHAPTER 3

For example, the chances of the Big Bang resulting in a universe, and our planet that can support life, are very small. Even those scientists who are atheists have been surprised by this.

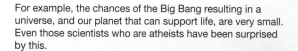

See pages 74-75 of the **Study Guide**

Briefing Sheet Session 1: The Big Bang

How did the universe start?

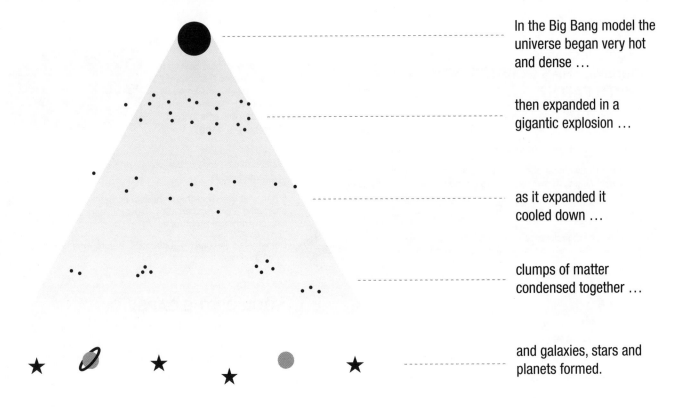

In the Big Bang model the universe began very hot and dense …

then expanded in a gigantic explosion …

as it expanded it cooled down …

clumps of matter condensed together …

and galaxies, stars and planets formed.

In the 1920s, Edwin Hubble discovered that the universe is still expanding. Astronomers detect that all the galaxies are moving away from us, and that more distant galaxies are moving away faster. This relationship between distance and speed means that the universe as a whole is expanding. In the 1990s, astronomers found that the expansion rate is not constant but is speeding up over time. Using the current best measure of expansion rate and how it changes over time, astronomers calculate that the universe itself must have begun about 13.5–13.9 billion years ago.

In 1965, Arno Penzias and Robert Wilson detected faint noise in a radio receiver. Further study showed that these radio waves arrive at earth from all directions, so the radiation must be coming from the universe itself. And the radiation has a thermal signature, showing that it was emitted by something hot. It is the light and heat of the Big Bang. Because of the expansion, the radiation has cooled over time to near absolute zero, consistent with predictions made before it was discovered.

How old is the universe?

Astronomers are able to measure age using several methods. Here are two of them:

Astronomers can calculate how long it will take a star to burn out, based on its size. Big stars burn faster than small stars. A 'globular cluster' is a cluster of stars (of different sizes) that formed at the same time. Since the big stars die out first, when only small stars are left scientists can tell that it is an old cluster. So by looking at the size of stars still in the cluster, astronomers can measure its age. The oldest globular clusters found are at least 11 billion years old. The universe as a whole must, therefore, be older than this.

With the Hubble Telescope astronomers can see light that has travelled for about 13.3 billion years, from the very first stars. The universe must be older than this for the light to reach us today.

For further information read: **http://map.gsfc.nasa.gov/universe**

Briefing Sheet Session 1: Fine-tuning

" The laws of nature have certain constants, and it's not clear why those constants have the values that they do. But it is clear that you can **change those constants a little bit**, and you would have **a universe that's no longer fertile for life**, you'd basically have a sterile universe.

Ard Louis, *Test of Faith* Part 1 [Time code: 17 min. 19]

" **Our universe** is very particular, **very special** in its character. There's a sense in which the universe was pregnant with life, essentially from the Big Bang onwards, because the very … physical fabric of the world, the laws of nature that science assumes … had to take **a very precise, very finely tuned form** for carbon-based life to be possible.

John Polkinghorne, *Test of Faith* Part 1 [Time code: 17 min. 44]

" The really important thing is that **the world as we observe it corresponds with what Christians would say the world ought to be like** … there's a correspondence between the theory and the observation.

Alister McGrath, *Test of Faith* Part 1 [Time code: 18 min. 41]

Fine-tuning, or the Anthropic Principle, is the idea that the universe is fined-tuned for life. There are many different factors that have to be exactly right – otherwise we would not be here. These details have amazed scientists of all religions and none because there is currently no good scientific explanation for why they should all be 'set' at such precise values. Here are just a few examples:

1. **Carbon** is an essential element for life. The **strong nuclear force** holds the particles that make carbon together. If the strong nuclear force were any weaker, carbon would never form. If it were any stronger, all the carbon would turn into oxygen. As it is, this balance is tuned exactly so that both elements are present.

2. The number of dimensions in our universe is right for life. You can only have planets with stable orbits if you have three dimensions in space. Any more than three and things would become very unstable, and we could not survive.

3. The amount of **matter** and **energy** present at the time of the Big Bang had to be very finely balanced. If this balance had not been exactly right, the universe would either have collapsed as soon as it began because of the strength of gravity or it would have blown apart too quickly. The probability of this balance occurring was about 1 in 10^{60} (one with sixty zeros after it).

4. In the universe, **disorder** always increases. The universe must have been much more ordered when it began in order for it to be as organized as it is now. Roger Penrose, a former professor of mathematics at Oxford, calculated that the chance that our universe would have this amount of order randomly is one in ten to the power of 10^{123}. This number is so large that if you were to write a zero on every atom in the visible universe, you would run out of atoms before you ran out of zeros.

5. **Gravity** would cause the universe to collapse, but there is a force called the **cosmological constant** that works against gravity. The cosmological constant has to have a very precise value so that the universe can be stable. If it were any greater, all the matter in the universe would be torn apart very quickly. If it were smaller, the universe would collapse.

6. Atoms are made up of **protons** and **electrons**. The mass of a proton must be almost exactly 1840 times the mass of an electron in order for the building blocks of life, such as DNA, to exist and be stable.

Briefing Sheet Session 1: Scientists and Faith through History

Thomas Huxley

" What Thomas Huxley saw in Darwinism was the potential to make biology scientific, to give it a significant public profile and to make science … important in society in a way in which it wasn't. Part of that meant, in a sense, prizing science from the hands of the clergy who, for various reasons, had tended to dominate scientific positions and the scientific establishment for quite a long time. The strategy he [Huxley] used, you might call it a kind of wedge strategy, was to say, "actually science and religion are different activities, they're in conflict. Clergy, hands off the science, leave it to the true professionals."

Peter Harrison, Test of Faith Part 1 [Time code: 5 min. 51]

Thomas Huxley was a British biologist in the 1800s. He was a friend and admirer of Charles Darwin and was a key spokesperson for Darwin's theory of evolution by natural selection.

Many of the people doing science in the 1800s were church ministers. Huxley and eight of his friends formed a dinner group and called themselves the 'X-Club'. The purpose of the group was to promote science and see it established as a profession supported by public funding. The members of the X-Club were mostly 'philosophical naturalists' – people who did not particularly believe in God, but who looked for inspiration in nature. In fact, Huxley came up with the word 'agnostic' (someone who does not think there is enough proof about God to decide whether God is real or not).

Huxley and the X-club promoted the idea that Christianity and science had always been in conflict because they wanted to establish a new professional scientific community free of clerical influence. Several best-selling books, which pushed the idea of 'warfare' between science and religion, popularized this account. Despite three hundred years of co-operation between religion and science, they created a myth of conflict that people still believe. Today, some scientists still use this story to argue against religion.

" Perhaps science wouldn't have emerged in the West at all, had it not been for a certain set of religious convictions about how the world was … the very idea that the world is a place that is rationally intelligible springs from – or at least for these people* it sprang from – the idea that there was a God who had put this order in place.

Peter Harrison, Test of Faith Part 1 [Time code: 3 min. 50]

(*The key figures in the development of science, most of whom had significant religious commitments.)

Scientists of faith

Roger Bacon (c. 1214–94)

Roger Bacon was a Franciscan monk who was important right at the beginning of the development of modern science. He believed it was very important to have an empirical (observed or based on experiment) basis for beliefs about the natural world. He contributed to the idea of 'laws of nature'. He studied mathematics, optics, the making of gunpowder, astronomy, and the anatomy of the eye and brain.

Johannes Kepler (1571–1630)

Johannes Kepler was an astronomer who formulated the laws of planetary motion that were based on the observations of Tycho Brahe. These are still used to calculate the approximate position of artificial satellites, the outer planets and smaller asteroids. He also did a lot of work in the field of optics and invented a new type of telescope which was used to confirm the discoveries of Galileo.

Galileo Galilee (1564–1642)

Galileo Galilee was one of the early supporters of a sun-centred (heliocentric) view of the solar system. He was censured and imprisoned by the church, but this was mostly because of the way he spoke to people in power. His imprisonment was house arrest, and he was never tortured (as Huxley would have had us believe). He never abandoned his faith and contributed to many areas of science including our understanding of the physics of motion and sound.

Michael Faraday (1791–1867)

Michael Faraday was a chemist and physicist and also an elder in his church. He established the basis for the electromagnetic field concept, electromagnetic induction, and established that electromagnetism could affect rays of light. He discovered benzene and invented the first working electric motors. Some people think he was the greatest experimenter in the history of science.

James Clerk Maxwell (1831–79)

James Clerk Maxwell was a physicist who formulated classical electromagnetic theory in 'Maxwell's equations', which synthesized all of the previously unrelated work regarding electricity, magnetism and light into one coherent theory. He demonstrated that electricity and magnetism travel in waves at the speed of light. He also created a statistical way to understand the kinetic motion of gases and laid the foundation for special relativity. Many scientists think that he was as important as Einstein and Newton.

Gregor Mendel (1822–84)

Gregor Mendel was an Augustinian priest and is known as the 'Father of Genetics'. He studied inherited traits in pea plants and discovered that inheritance follows certain laws. His work went largely unappreciated until the turn of the twentieth century.

Briefing Sheet Session 2: An Accident in the Making?

CHAPTER 1

Some evolutionary biologists say that the world is without design or purpose. They think that it came into being through a meaningless process, ruled by random chance.

The Bible says that we are made in God's image.

ARE THE BIBLE AND SCIENCE OPPOSED TO EACH OTHER?

Some people are sceptical of anything that predicts a very old age for the earth, and of evolutionary theory.

And some say that living things could not have evolved without any intervention by an intelligent being. They claim that the world was created by an 'Intelligent Designer'.

CHAPTER 2

But others say that evolution doesn't have to lead to atheism.

They say that Genesis was meant to be interpreted as an important but not scientific message.

And that you can see reliable evidence for common ancestors in our DNA.

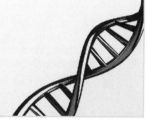

CHAPTER 4

But evolution has other challenges for faith – **what about the suffering and death that are part of the process?**

This is the toughest question for Christians in this area.

Some think that the process of producing fruitful life through evolution is a fitting way for God – who loves and gives his people freedom – to create.

Is disease a necessary product of a creation that is able to have life in such variety?

What we *do* know is the good news of the New Testament …

… and that science cannot make paradise on earth. We know that it can be misused, because human brings are flawed creatures.

CHAPTER 3

Some people say that evolution is a **totally chance** process – like the **random** throw of a dice – at odds with a purposeful God.

But random can mean two things:

1. In day-to-day life we use it to mean "purposeless".

2. In a scientific sense it means that the microscopic details of a process may be unpredictable – but **the overall process may be very predictable**.

So although evolution may appear random, it may be the best way of finding solutions to biological 'problems'.

In fact, the Professor of Paleobiology, Simon Conway Morris, believes that evolution can only go in a very few directions – and if you started the process again from scratch, you would end up with very similar things – which fits with the idea that **we were meant to be here**.

CHAPTER 5

THE COMMAND GIVEN IN GENESIS WAS NOT TO FIGURE OUT EXACTLY HOW THE WORLD WAS CREATED, BUT TO LOOK AFTER IT.

What we know about climate change must move us to action.

People in the West have benefited from cheap energy in the past. They have a moral duty to reduce their own consumption and help developing countries to develop in sustainable ways.

That change must start with the human heart.

Briefing Sheet Session 2: Views on Genesis 1

GOD IS CREATOR

1

We should read Genesis 1 as a historical and scientific, common-sense statement of the facts.

The six days in Genesis are twenty-four hours long, so in total God created the world in 144 hours, about 10,000 years ago.

This is the only way to take the Bible seriously. The Sabbath commandment in Exodus that refers to the creation week, and the genealogy of Jesus in Luke, support this view.

Advocates of this view look for scientific evidence that the earth is much younger than mainstream science claims, and that evolution cannot have happened.

This view is incompatible with modern mainstream science and says that mainstream science has interpreted the evidence wrongly because of false assumptions about the physical laws (i.e., that they are always the same through time and space).

For example, there is the idea that small changes may have taken place in animal populations (microevolution) but new species could never form, and that gaps in the fossil record back this up.

ASSUME MIRACLES IN CREATION

2

The 'days' of Genesis 1 refer to long periods of time. The Hebrew word yom has as many different meanings as 'day' does in English. Hebrew does not have a word for a long period of time (era, epoch etc.), so yom was used instead.

The biblical support for this view comes from the seventh day of God's activity, which is never said to end. This is used by Jesus to clarify the Sabbath law and as a theological theme about heaven by the author of Hebrews. In addition, Scripture teaches that 'for God a day is like a thousand years,' showing that God measures time differently than we do.

In this view, the events of natural history happened in the order given in Genesis 1, but were stretched out over much longer periods of time. This is consistent with the billions-of-years time frame of mainstream science, but the order of events is somewhat different. God miraculously intervened at some points during the development of creation, such as the creation of plants or birds. (These were not created in the order suggested by evolutionary biology.)

VERY OLD UNIVERSE, LONG TIME SCALE OF CREATION

3

There are different types of literature in the Bible: history, songs, poems, parables, etc. Genesis 1 should be interpreted with an eye for literary devices such as repetition and figurative language, and with an understanding of cultural, historical and biblical context.

For example, the sun and moon are not called by their proper names, because these names also referred to gods in the surrounding pagan cultures. Instead, they are called 'big lamp' and 'small lamp' to emphasize that there is only one God. The narrative is structured around God creating spaces by separating things, then filling those spaces:

SEPARATION	FILLING
Day 1, Light and darkness	Day 4, Sun and moon
Day 2, Sky and sea	Day 5, Birds and fish
Day 3, Sea and dry land	Day 6, Animals and humans

In this view, Genesis is not a scientific text. We should look first at what the text meant to the first audience to learn its non-scientific message (the 'who' and 'why'), then at modern science to understand how and when God created the universe, the earth and life.

Briefing Sheet Session 2: Is there Purpose in Evolution?

> *Converge*
>
> 1. *To come together from different directions so as eventually to meet.*
> 2. *Converge on/upon: to come from different directions and meet at.*

Stephen Jay Gould was a world-class palaeontologist and writer of some very popular science books. He didn't believe in God, and he thought that evolution was a purposeless, undirected process. He thought that if you 're-ran the tape of life', and let evolution happen all over again, you would end up with something very different:

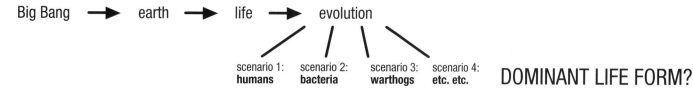

Simon Conway Morris worked on the same type of fossils as Stephen Jay Gould (from the Burgess Shale in British Columbia, Canada) and came to a very different conclusion. **He thinks that there are only so many ways that the process of evolution (on any planet) could 'make' things.** The evidence he points to is '**convergence**'.

For example, there were very similar sorts of animals in North America and Australia (some now extinct) – with one important difference. The North American versions were placental mammals, and the Australians were marsupials (with pouches like kangaroos). So there were marsupial moles, flying squirrels, wolves, mice and, in South America, marsupial sabre-toothed cats.

What does this show? These two types of animals evolved independently but acquired very similar characteristics. So the process of evolution is not completely random but converges on certain solutions to a problem (of how to 'make' effective diggers, treetop dwellers, or predators).

It could look as if things were meant to be that way ...? Is it on purpose?

> " The general received wisdom is that **evolution is completely open-ended. It can go in any direction you like**. And at first sight that seems entirely reasonable, because biology – evolution – seems to be largely without any underlying laws. So leading from that there is then a metaphysical assumption which says that all things are equally probable, but also everything is accidental: it could be this, it could be that. Whereas **my view is the exact reverse, that the roads of evolution are well defined, and evolution can go in only a very few directions** in comparison to the immense plenitude which the neo-Darwinian would suggest.

> " Effectively it is arguing that from different starting positions, some sort of structure emerges which is remarkably similar. In other words, I go to an aquarium, I see an octopus in the tank. I look at the octopus, and she glances back at me. The eye in my head is constructed on what we call a camera principle. The eye in the octopus' head is constructed effectively the same way; it's also a camera eye. Now we know enough from molecular biology, from the fossil record, and evolution generally, that the common ancestor – and indeed we do have a common ancestor with the octopus – lived about 500 million years ago in the Cambrian, and could not possibly have possessed that sort of camera eye. So **independently the ancestors of the octopus, and the ancestors of Simon Conway Morris, generation by generation, evolved a system which is extremely effective for seeing, called the 'camera eye'.** So that's just one example of convergence. It goes a bit further than that because this camera eye has actually evolved independently, I think, about seven times, so you almost get the sense that there are stable points in biological space towards which things can navigate.

> Professor Simon Conway Morris, *Test of Faith* Part 2 [Time code: 15 min. 53]

Further Reading

Simon Conway Morris, 'Extraterrestrials: Aliens like Us?'
http://adsabs.harvard.edu/abs/2005A&G....46d..24M

Simon Conway Morris (ed.), *The Deep Structure of Biology: Is Convergence Sufficiently Ubiquitous to Give a Directional Signal?* (Templeton Foundation Press, 2008)

Simon Conway Morris, *Life's Solution: Inevitable Humans in a Lonely Universe* (Cambridge University Press, 2003)

Simon Conway Morris, *The Crucible of Creation* (Oxford University Press, 1998)

Briefing Sheet Session 2: Views on Genesis 2 and 3

This sheet outlines the different ways that the biblical account of the creation of humankind and the scientific account of human evolution might relate to each other. Christians may well hold views that combine elements of several of these. The Adam and Eve narrative sets the scene for the fall, so view A on the fall goes with view A on Adam and Eve, and so on.

Genesis 2: Who were Adam and Eve?

A. We should read Genesis 1 as a historical and scientific, common sense, statement of the facts. God created Adam and Eve miraculously on the sixth day of creation.

B. We should read Genesis 1 as a historical and scientific, common sense, statement of the facts. God intervened in a miraculous way at several points in evolutionary history, including at the creation of two human beings: Adam and Eve.

C. While the early chapters of Genesis are not a historical document in the modern sense, they do refer to events that really happened. But they happened in the culture and place Genesis describes. God chose a couple of Neolithic farmers (Adam and Eve) in the ancient Near East (or maybe a community of farmers) and revealed himself to them in a special way, bringing them into fellowship with himself. They were representative of all humankind, as the first people God brought into relationship with himself.

D. As in Model C, while the early chapters of Genesis are not a historical document, they do refer to events that really happened. Among early humans, there was a growing awareness of God's presence and calling upon their lives to which they responded in obedience and worship.

E. Genesis 1 should be interpreted with an eye for literary devices such as repetition and figurative language. There is no historical connection between the theological and biological stories. The question of the birth of the first spiritually alive humans is essentially unanswerable. The purpose of the early chapters of Genesis is to give a theological account of the role and importance of humankind in God's purposes.

Genesis 3: Views on the fall

A. There was no death at all before the fall. When Adam and Eve disobeyed God not only did they die spiritually, but there were also big changes in the way creation operates. From that point on, decay and the physical deaths of animals, plants and humans were possible.

B. Until the fall, Adam and Eve were immortal. When they disobeyed God they died spiritually, and later physically. The physical deaths of animals and plants were already occurring.

C. Adam and Eve (or the group of people God chose) disobeyed him. This act of disobedience separated them from God and they died spiritually. Because these people were representative of all humankind, everyone else fell too. The physical deaths of humans happened throughout evolutionary history.

D. The fall was a conscious rejection of the growing awareness of God's calling. It led to spiritual death. The physical deaths of humans happened throughout evolutionary history.

E. This is the eternal story of us all. It is a theological account that describes the common experience of separation from God through disobedience to God's commands. The result for us is spiritual death. The physical deaths of humans happened throughout evolutionary history.

Briefing Sheet Session 2: The Science behind Climate Change

(Based, with permission, on the JRI briefing paper by Sir John Houghton, 'Global Warming, Climate Change and Sustainability: Challenge to Scientists, Policy-makers and Christians' [2007] **www.jri.org.uk**)

'Greenhouse gases' in the earth's atmosphere such as water vapour, carbon dioxide or methane, trap heat and keep the earth warm. This 'greenhouse effect' keeps the earth 20 – 30°C warmer than it would otherwise be and is essential for our survival. But the greenhouse effect is increasing. We have a record of what the weather was like in the past, and of the gases in the air at that time, preserved for us in the ice caps in Greenland and the Antarctic. Scientists can drill down through the layers of ice that have built up over thousands of years and analyse the bubbles of gas trapped in each layer. From this we can see that, since the beginning of the industrial revolution in the 1750s, the amount of carbon dioxide in the atmosphere has increased by nearly 40%. With chemical analysis we can see that this is mostly because of the burning of fossil fuels (coal, oil and gas).

The average temperature on earth has risen over the last century. There is strong evidence that most of this rise has been caused by the increase in greenhouse gases, and especially carbon dioxide. Scientists predict that, during the twenty-first century, the average temperature will rise by 2 – 6°C. This doesn't sound like very much, but the difference in average

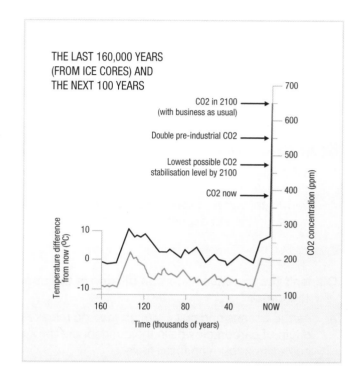

THE LAST 160,000 YEARS (FROM ICE CORES) AND THE NEXT 100 YEARS

temperature between the middle of an ice age and a warm period is only about 5 – 6°C. The predicted temperature rise could have a huge impact.

As water heats it expands, so as temperatures continue to increase the sea level will rise, flooding low-lying coastal areas around the world. The temperature changes already produced by humans will take hundreds of years to feed into the deep ocean, so the sea level will continue to rise for hundreds of years even if we stopped producing any more greenhouse gases overnight. Warmer temperatures will also cause greater evaporation of fresh water on land, leading to more water vapour in the atmosphere and more rain or snow. This will cause drought in some areas and flooding in others. There is no evidence that hurricanes will become more common, but it is possible that they will become more severe as the surface temperature of the sea increases.

All of these changes in the weather will affect the ability of humans, plants and animals to survive. The worst impact will be felt in developing countries. In the short term, crop yields will increase in colder countries, but the damaging effects in warm countries, flooding and storms will far outweigh these

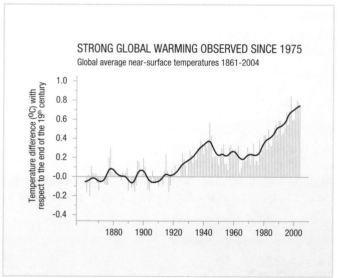

STRONG GLOBAL WARMING OBSERVED SINCE 1975
Global average near-surface temperatures 1861-2004

Met office Hadley centre

advantages. Eventually crop yields will decrease worldwide as temperatures increase further. If we cut down our production of greenhouse gases now, the harmful effects will be greatly reduced. It has been argued that developed countries, which have benefited from burning huge amounts of fossil fuels, should make the biggest efforts to cut down and allow developing countries to continue to develop.

Briefing Sheet Session 2: Climate Change Questions

(Adapted with permission from 'Climate Change Controversies: A Simple Guide', The Royal Society [2007] **http://royalsociety.org**)

Q1: The earth's climate always varies. Aren't we just in a natural period of warming?

A: The earth's climate varies due to many different factors, including cycles of ice ages caused by changes in the distance between the earth and the sun, volcanic eruptions and changes in the sun itself. However, none of these factors is enough to explain the rapid changes in the last 100 years.

Q2: There isn't enough carbon dioxide in the atmosphere to cause any significant change, is there?

A: Although there isn't a big volume of carbon dioxide (CO_2) in the atmosphere, it can have a significant effect. It has a direct effect because it traps heat very strongly. It also has an indirect effect because, as the earth warms up, water evaporates more quickly from lakes and the sea. This increases the amount of water vapour in the atmosphere, which causes an even stronger greenhouse effect.

Q3: Isn't the increase in carbon dioxide in the atmosphere the result of climate change, rather than the cause?

A: As the oceans and soil warm up they do release carbon dioxide into the atmosphere. Scientists can find the origin of carbon dioxide in the atmosphere through chemical analysis. Most of the increase in CO_2 levels comes from burning fossil fuels.

Q4: I thought that the observations of weather balloons and satellites were inaccurate?

A: In the early 1990s there were errors both in the way that data was collected and in the way it was analysed. These errors have been corrected, and now the data from weather balloons and satellites agrees with data collected by other methods.

Q5: Aren't computer models of the climate inaccurate?

A: Although the climate is very complex, scientists have been able to create increasingly accurate models of the way it works. These computer models have been used to simulate changes in the climate over the course of the last century, and their simulations have matched what actually happened. Using these models scientists can give general predictions about the course of the climate in the future on a global scale, based on different predictions about human behaviour.

Q6: Isn't climate change caused by the sun becoming more active?

A: The sun's activity does play a role in shaping climate. However, that alone is not enough to explain the recent warming. Also, there has been very little change in the sun's activity over the last three decades, so this cannot account for the observed warming.

Q7: Surely it's not a big deal. Aren't climate scientists exaggerating?

A: The earth's ecosystems are very finely balanced. Even a change of 2 – 3°C would be greater than has been seen for ten thousand years, and many species would find it very difficult to adapt. The people most affected will be those in developing countries and the poor, creating greater inequalities in access to food, clean water, and medical treatment.

Briefing Sheet Session 3: Is Anybody There?

CHAPTER 1

Some scientists claim that we run on rails determined by our physical characteristics, and that spiritual experiences are just a by-product of our brains.

But neuroscientists who are also Christians believe that we are made in the image of God.

> **When we are having a religious experience, something happens in our brains.**
>
> But that doesn't prove that religious experience is **just** what is in our brain. The experience also means something too.

> And it is possible to artificially stimulate certain parts of the brain, and make someone feel angry or sad.
>
> But that doesn't mean that it isn't possible to feel happy or sad for genuine reasons!

CHAPTER 2

We are not just determined by our biology.

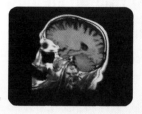

Our experiences and the environment we live in also play a role in shaping who we are.

And these scientists believe that the brain is more than the sum of its parts.

You could say that **our minds and personalities emerge from the complex structure of the brain**.

But they can't be defined by just looking at the cells in the brain.

> It's like music that emerges from the strings of an instrument – it can be described in a mechanical way, but it has a much deeper meaning than vibrations of strings.

CHAPTER 4

To really understand things in a meaningful way, theology and neuroscience need to talk to each other.

We need to read both the book of the Bible and the book of nature and not be afraid of asking new questions.

We need to use the tools of **both** faith and science to explore the world.

And **for Christians science increases their sense of wonder at what God has created.**

CHAPTER 3

With genetic technology, we now have the ability to enhance or even clone ourselves.

But **even a genetic clone would be more than the sum of its DNA**.

We are creative	We have the ability for moral reasoning	We make meaningful choices

These abilities seem to go far beyond our biological makeup.

See pages 94-95 of the **Study Guide**

Briefing Sheet Session 3: When Does Human Life Begin?

Below is a summary of the main views held on the status of the early embryo and the arguments that people use to defend them.

A) Human life begins at fertilization *(0–6 hours)*

Biblical/theological arguments

- The Bible names Jesus and other people by this stage.
- This is the origin of a 'personal history'.
- This is when Jesus became incarnate as a man.
- Relationship with God is established.
- In the Bible the Hebrews believed life began as soon as they were aware of it being there. The message is that life begins as soon as there is something there. With our knowledge today, this means conception.

Biological arguments

- Fertilization provides a fairly precise moment of beginning.
- The genetic make-up of the individual is specified during this stage.

B) Human life begins at implantation *(7–10 days)*

Biblical/theological arguments

- Physical relationship with the mother begins – she can become aware of her pregnancy. Part of what defines us as human is being in relationship.
- Twinning may occur between the 'blastocyst' (hollow ball of cells) stage and implantation, so until implantation there isn't 'one' individual present to relate to God.
- This is what passages about the unborn refer to because this is the time when pre-scientific societies became aware of pregnancy.

Biological arguments

- There is a high rate of embryo loss before implantation (70–80%).
- Until implantation, it is impossible to tell what parts will become the embryo and what will become the placenta.

C) Human life begins at the primitive streak stage *(14 days)*

Biological argument

- The development of the primitive streak marks where the nervous system will begin to develop. The capacity for sensation and pain are important in defining humanness and in determining how we treat others.

D) The beginning of human life is a continual process

This is the view that all of the above 'milestones' are not that critical, since the development of human life is a continual process from fertilization through to birth and onwards. Human life deserves our care and protection all the way through, although prenatal care will increase in line with development.

Some Bible passages that are relevant to this discussion

These highlight the fact that human development is shaped and purposed by God from the beginning:

- Jesus' incarnation – Luke 1:31–33
- God establishes a relationship with Isaiah and Jeremiah before birth – Isaiah 49:5, Jeremiah 1:5
- God's knowledge of us in the womb – Psalm 139:13–16 and Job 10:8–12
- An important marker of new life was 'quickening', when a baby kicked for the first time – Luke 1:44
- Being in relationship is an important part of personhood – Genesis 2:18
- Care of pregnant women – Exodus 21:22–23

Appendix 3: Songs

The following songs and hymns fit in with the overall theme of the course, are reasonably well known, and should be relatively easy to sing without a strong musical accompaniment. We have given the first line (in brackets) and the songwriter. If you do not have copies of them, an internet search will usually find you the lyrics, guitar chords and a sound sample of the song – as well as any copyright information you need to be aware of when reproducing the song in a worship setting.

'All Creatures of our God and King', words by Francis of Assisi, tune by Peter von Brachel
(All creatures of our God and King, Lift up your voice and with us sing)

'Almighty God', Tim Hughes
(The rising Sun that fills the sky, The starry host that lights the night)

'Awesome God (Your Voice)', Vicky Beeching
(Your voice is the voice that commanded the universe to be. Your voice is the voice that is speaking words of love to me.)

'Everything that Has Breath', Matt Redman
(Let everything that, everything that, Everything that has breath praise the Lord)

'God of Wonders', Marc Byrd and Steve Hindalong
(Lord of all creation, of water, earth and sky)

'How Great is our God', Chris Tomlin
(The splendour of the King, Clothed in majesty)

'How Great Thou Art', Carl Gustav Boberg
(O Lord my God! When I in awesome wonder, Consider all the works Thy hands have made)

'Indescribable', Laura Story
(From the highest of heights, to the depths of the sea, Creation's revealing Your majesty)

'My Jesus, my Saviour', Darlene Zschech
(My Jesus, my saviour, Lord there is none like you)

'Who Paints the Skies (River of Fire)', Stuart Townend
(Who paints the skies into glorious day? Only the splendour of Jesus)

Appendix 4: Leading a Discussion Group

This course is designed for small groups. As we have said, the dynamics for a discussion are best if the group includes no more than 12 people. The larger the group, the longer discussion must go on for everyone to have a say, and the more difficult it is to lead – it can very quickly become overwhelming.

Break-out groups are a great idea, even in a fairly small gathering, if people are not very confident about taking part in discussion. If you are relying on a scientist to help with technical information, the entire group could be part of a Q&A session with this person before you break out into smaller groups.

In most groups people will have a wide variety of experiences and levels of confidence on these topics, so make sure that everyone has a chance to be to be involved. You may want to establish some ground rules for discussion. Whether you go over them with your group or just have them in mind as you lead is up to you:

- Be open-minded. If you already have an opinion, listen and see if you might learn something new.
- No question is stupid – with a variety of levels of experience in the group, everyone deserves a chance to understand the things being discussed.
- It's okay to question things – these are topics about which Christians hold different views, so don't be afraid to think about things from a different angle.
- Try to keep tangents to a minimum – some questions will have to be saved until later.
- One person talks at a time.
- One person shouldn't dominate the discussion.
- What's said should stay among the group members and not be passed on – for some who are exploring new ground this will be really important.
- The course material is serious and should be challenging, but it's important that the atmosphere is positive and inspiring. You can do this by choosing a variety of discussion questions (e.g., including some of the 'easy' level topics and some that focus on areas that will not be too controversial) as well as by using the Epilogue as an opportunity to return to familiar ground.
- Don't be afraid of silence – people need time to think.
- While it's easy for things to become heated, especially where issues are close to people's hearts, it's crucial that discussions remain civil.

You might have people in your group who would appreciate at least some activities that aren't group discussion, so here are a few suggestions:

- Spend more time on an Introduction or Epilogue activity and cut down the time you spend on discussion.
- Discuss a Short Question or part of a Discussion Topic in pairs or smaller groups.
- Ask for a volunteer to read a briefing sheet aloud (remember that not everyone will be confident reading aloud).
- Give the group time to silently read a briefing sheet, Bible passage or series of quotes.
- Get everyone to write down their answers to one or two questions (choose the sort of question about which everyone is likely to have an opinion). People could then share their answers with the group or in pairs.

Appendix 5: About the Writers

In 2005, Ruth Bancewicz and the directors of the Faraday Institute for Science and Religion began the Test of Faith project in response to the demand for user-friendly resources on science and faith for churches.

The Faraday Institute for Science and Religion

The Faraday Institute is an academic research enterprise based at St Edmund's College, Cambridge.

The Institute has four main activities:

1. Scholarly research and publication on science and religion, including the organization of invited groups of experts to write joint publications.
2. To provide short-term courses in science and religion.
3. To organize seminars and lectures on science and religion.
4. To provide accurate information on science and religion for the international media and wider public.

The Faraday Institute derives its name from Michael Faraday, one of Britain's best-known scientists, who saw his faith as integral to his scientific research.

The Faraday Institute has a Christian ethos but encourages engagement with a wide diversity of opinions concerning interactions between science and religion without engaging in advocacy. It aims to provide accurate information in order to facilitate informed debate.

Dr Ruth Bancewicz
Project Leader/Editor

Ruth has been a research associate at the Faraday Institute for Science and Religion since it was established in 2006. After studying Genetics at Aberdeen University she completed a PhD at Edinburgh University. This was followed by some postdoctoral research at the Wellcome Trust Centre for Cell Biology, Edinburgh University, and then she worked as the Development Officer for Christians in Science for three years before moving full-time to the Faraday Institute in 2007. Ruth is a member of City Church Cambridge (a Newfrontiers church), and in her spare time she can be found cooking for friends, enjoying the great outdoors, and (perhaps) proving that it's possible to take up ballet as an adult.

James Crocker
Research Assistant

James studied theology at the University of St Andrews. He has lived half his life in the United Kingdom and half in the United States. His interest in science-faith issues comes from being the son of a Church of England minister and a scientist.

This project was supported by a grant from the John Templeton Foundation. The opinions expressed in these materials are those of the authors, and do not necessarily reflect the views of the John Templeton Foundation.

Appendix 6: Biographies of the Scientists and Theologians Featured on the DVD

Note: 'Christians in Science' is a UK-based network of Christians working in or studying science, and of others who are interested in the interaction between the two. The 'American Scientific Affiliation' is a US-based fellowship of Christians working in science or related disciplines.

Dr Denis Alexander is the director of the Faraday Institute for Science and Religion at St Edmund's College, Cambridge, and is a popular writer and speaker on science and faith. His latest book is called *Creation or Evolution: Do We Have to Choose?* He is editor of the journal *Science & Christian Belief* and is on the National Committee of Christians in Science.

Until recently, Denis was the head of an immunology (the study of the immune system) lab at The Babraham Institute, Cambridge. He spent the first fifteen years of his working life developing science teaching and research in universities in Turkey and Lebanon, and was evacuated with his family from Beirut during the civil war in 1986. Denis is married to Tina and they have three children who have also inherited the travelling bug. He spends as much of his spare time as possible hiking in sunny countries.

Professor Katherine Blundell is an astrophysicist based at Oxford University. Her research is on the physics of active galaxies. She recently set up a project, 'Global Jet Watch', that will use telescopes based at schools around the world. The children will be able to keep a 24-hour watch on a 'microquasar' that fires off jets of hydrogen at high speeds. She speaks on science to lay audiences and on science-faith issues to a wide variety of audiences. Katherine is married to Professor Stephen Blundell, who is also based at Oxford University.

Professor John Bryant is a biologist based at Exeter University and has many years of experience in research on the biochemistry of genes. He also has a keen interest in bioethical issues. He introduced one of the first bioethics courses for biology students in a UK university and runs workshops for biologists on teaching ethics. He has co-authored a book explaining bioethical issues for Christian non-scientists as well as a textbook, *Introduction to Bioethics*, for university students.

John speaks frequently on issues in bioethics and in the science-religion debate. He also writes regularly on bioethics, both in a specifically Christian context and for 'secular' readerships. He was Chair of Christians in Science between 2001 and 2007 and President of the Society for Experimental Biology from 2003 to 2005. John is married to Marje, who is a counsellor, and they have two children and three grandchildren. He loves mountains, marshes and other wild places and enjoys bird-watching. He is a keen runner, a Bob Dylan fan and supports Crystal Palace football club.

Rev Dr Alasdair Coles is a lecturer in neuroimmunology (study of the nervous and immune system together) at Cambridge University and an honorary consultant neurologist to Addenbrooke's and Hinchingbrooke Hospitals. He is involved in research into new treatments for multiple sclerosis (a disease that causes damage to the nerves).

His amateur research interest, in the neurological basis for religious experience, came from managing a small cohort of patients with spiritual experiences due to temporal lobe epilepsy (seizures in the parts of the brain that are involved in speech, memory and hearing). He has given lectures on this subject at several universities. Alasdair was ordained in the Church of England in 2008 and is now a curate at St Andrews Church, Cambridge, alongside his medical and scientific work. Alasdair is married to Olivia and they have two young children.

Dr Francis Collins was the director of the Human Genome Project (the international initiative to decode the DNA instruction manual that's inside each of our cells) in the USA until 2008. His PhD was in quantum mechanics (the physics of atoms and subatomic particles), but he later qualified as a medical doctor and went into research on genetic diseases. His research has led to the identification of the genes that are affected in cystic fibrosis, neurofibromatosis, Huntington's disease and diabetes. He is a member of the U.S. National Academy of Sciences.

Francis grew up on a farm in Virginia among a creative and theatrical family and was on the stage at the age of four. He was taught at home until he was ten and then discovered science through a charismatic chemistry teacher at high school. He became a Christian during his medical studies and is now involved in speaking and writing on science and faith. His book *The Language of God* was a New York Times bestseller. He is married to Diane Baker, a leader in the genetic counseling community, and has two grown children.

Professor Simon Conway Morris is a palaeobiologist (someone who studies fossils and their origin, growth and structure). His most recent research is on the evolution of characteristics or structures, such as the eye, which have emerged independently in different organisms (convergent evolution). He often speaks on the philosophical implications of these patterns in the history of evolution, and he has written two books looking at the science of convergent evolution and what it means for us.

Simon was brought up in London and studied at Bristol and then Cambridge University. He has held various academic and research positions at Cambridge and the Open University, and he was elected to a chair in Evolutionary Palaeobiology at Cambridge University in 1995. He is married to Zoë, and they have two children. If undisturbed, he can usually be found reading G.K. Chesterton, with a glass of wine nearby.

Catherine Cutler is a horticulturalist who is passionate about care for the environment. She is horticultural supervisor at the Eden Project, an environmental park and educational centre in Cornwall. She studied horticulture at Wye College, the University of London. Following this she spent some time in Borneo working on a project called 'Forests Absorbing Carbon Dioxide', where she and others were trying to re-establish native tree species in Borneo to those areas being cut down for forestry. She then worked for the Royal Horticultural Society before joining the Eden Project.

Catherine is married to Mike, and they have one child. In her spare time she is to be found being active in creative ways – namely gardening, glass fusing or card making.

Dr William A. (Bill) Dembski is a mathematician and philosopher. His first degree was in psychology, and since then he has achieved PhDs in mathematics and philosophy as well as postgraduate studies in divinity. He is now teaching at Southwestern Baptist Theological Seminary in the USA. He is a senior fellow of the Discovery Institute, the leading Intelligent Design research and education centre in Seattle.

Bill is the author of many books and has won numerous prizes for his work. He has been very involved in the Intelligent Design movement, taking part in numerous conferences, lectures and debates. His other interests include lifting weights, shooting guns and wrestling with his kids. He is married to Jana, and they have three children – Chloe, John and Will.

Dr Deborah Haarsma is Associate Professor in the Department of Physics and Astronomy at Calvin College in Grand Rapids. She studied both physics and music as an undergraduate and received a Bachelor of Science in Physics and a Bachelor of Music in Piano Performance. This was followed by a PhD in astrophysics at the Massachusetts Institute of Technology. Her current research is on galaxy formation and galaxy clusters.

Deborah often speaks on science and faith to a variety of audiences and has recently co-written a book entitled *Origins: A Reformed Look at Creation, Design, and Evolution* that aims to help those in the church understand the issues. She is married to Loren Haarsma, who is also a physics professor at Calvin College, and they are active in their church. She enjoys reading science fiction and Jane Austen, and recently took up running.

Professor Peter Harrison is Andreas Idreos Professor of Science and Religion at the University of Oxford. His main research interest is the impact of religion on the history of science. Peter was born in Australia and studied Science and Arts at the University of Queensland. He was a high school science teacher until he developed an interest in the philosophy of science and religion. He studied philosophy and religion at Yale University and then completed a PhD in religious history. Before taking up his post at Oxford he was Professor of History and Philosophy at Bond University, Australia. He speaks regularly in public lectures on the history of science and religion.

Peter is married to Carol, and they have two children.

Sir John Houghton is a climate scientist who has been working in the field for many decades. He has been involved in research and public policy decisions in both the UK and at the United Nations. He was Professor of Atmospheric Physics at Oxford University until 1983, where he pioneered new ways of observing the earth from space. He was Director General of the 'Met office', the UK's weather forecasting and climate research centre, for eight years. He has been closely involved in the scientific evaluation of climate change and chaired the Scientific Assessment panel for the Intergovernmental Panel on Climate Change until 2002.

John has given a lot of time to speaking and writing on the issues of climate change, and also on the relationship between Christianity and science. He is currently the President of the John Ray Initiative, a charity that connects environment, science and Christianity, and is a vice-president of Christians in Science. He is married to Sheila and they live in Wales, where they enjoy mountain walking and sailing. They have two children and seven grandchildren.

Professor Ian Hutchinson is a physicist at the Massachusetts Institute of Technology (MIT) and is head of MIT's department of Nuclear Science and Engineering. He and his research group are leaders in exploring the confinement, using strong magnetic fields, of plasmas hotter than the sun's centre, aimed at producing energy from controlled nuclear fusion reactions.

Ian has written and spoken widely on science and Christianity and is a member of the MIT Christian Faculty Fellowship. When not at work he enjoys music and sings baritone/tenor with the Newton Choral Society. His sporting enthusiasms include hiking, fly fishing and squash. He is married to Fran, and they have two children.

Test of Faith – Appendix 6: Biographies of the Scientists and Theologians Featured on the DVD **117**
www.testoffaith.com

APPENDICES

Dr Ard Louis is a theoretical physicist based at Oxford University. He leads an interdisciplinary research group studying problems on the border between physics, chemistry and biology. Until recently he was based in the Chemistry department at Cambridge University. He is the International Secretary for Christians in Science and an associate of the Faraday Institute for Science and Religion.

Ard was born in the Netherlands but raised in Gabon, Central Africa, and he maintains an active interest in international students and development issues. He is on the board of Arca Associates, an international development organization. He is married to Mary. In his spare time he can be found cooking for friends, enjoying fine wines or scuba diving.

Professor Alister McGrath is currently Professor of Theology, Ministry and Education and Head of the Centre for Theology, Religion and Culture at King's College, London. He originally studied chemistry at Oxford University, followed by research in molecular biophysics at Oxford while studying for a theology degree at the same time. After further study at Cambridge, he was ordained into the Anglican Church. He spent several years in parish ministry before heading back to Oxford as a tutor at Wycliffe Hall, eventually becoming Professor of Historical Theology at Oxford University.

Much of Alister's research, writing and speaking has been on science and theology, and he has responded vigorously to Richard Dawkins' book *The God Delusion,* both in print and in debate. He is married to Joanna Collicutt-McGrath, and they have two children. When not writing, he enjoys reading detective novels and hill walking.

Professor Bill Newsome is a Neurobiologist at Stanford University School of Medicine. His research is on visual perception – the way that the brain processes messages from the eyes. He grew up in north Florida and studied Physics at Stetson University. He went on to complete a PhD at the California Institute of Technology, where he began his work on visual perception.

Bill speaks regularly on the relationship between science and faith and on the impact of neuroscience on our understanding of the mind. He is a member of the National Academy of Sciences and is the faculty sponsor of the Intervarsity Christian Fellowship graduate student group at Stanford. In his spare time he enjoys birding, landscape photography and reading history.

Dr Cherith Fee Nordling is a theologian with a background in pastoral care and counselling. She worked in law for twelve years before returning to university to study theology – first at Regent College in Canada, and then she completed a PhD at the University of St Andrews in Scotland. She has spent time at Calvin College, teaching and setting up spiritual development programmes through Bible study, mentoring and other activities along with her husband and others. She has also taught theology at Regent College, Calvin Theological Seminary, Wheaton College and Kuyper College.

Cherith is married to musician Robert Nordling, has two sons at university and relies on Digory, their Welsh terrier, to keep everything running smoothly. She is a classic film buff, shares detective novels with her parents and loves to walk the beach anytime, anywhere.

Rev Dr John Polkinghorne's first career was in particle physics, and he was made Professor of Mathematical Physics at Cambridge University in 1979. He resigned at the age of forty-eight to become ordained in the Anglican Church. After several years as a parish priest he returned to Cambridge University to work in the field of science and religion. He was then made President of Queens College, Cambridge, where he took part in both chapel and academic life.

He has written a huge number of books on science and faith and is a popular speaker. John was married to Ruth, who sadly passed away in 2006. He has three children and nine grandchildren.

Paul Taylor is the Senior Speaker for Answers in Genesis (UK/Europe), an organization that promotes Young Earth Creationism. He was born in Ashton-under-Lyne in Lancashire and grew up in Stalybridge. He learned to play the piano early in life and was educated at Chetham's School of Music, Manchester. An interest in science took him to Nottingham University to study chemistry, and he was a science teacher for seventeen years.

Paul became a Christian in his early teens and was soon convinced of the scientific and historical nature of the early chapters of Genesis. He has written four books and now frequently travels to speak on this interpretation of Genesis. He is married to Geraldene, and they have five children.

Rev Dr David Wilkinson trained first as a scientist and then as a theologian. His first PhD was in astrophysics, looking at the process of star and galaxy formation, and mass extinctions. After this he studied theology at Cambridge and became a Methodist minister. Later he completed a PhD in theology and since then has held a number of different positions at Durham University in apologetics and theology. He is now Principal of St John's College and Lecturer in the Department of Theology and Religion, Durham University.

He is interested in current culture and has written books relating subjects such as 'The X-Files' and *Star Wars* to Christianity, as well as a number of other popular level books. He is committed to Newcastle United, 'The Simpsons' and Bob Dylan. He is married to Alison, and they have two children.

Dr Jennifer Wiseman grew up on a cattle ranch in Arkansas, where she learned to appreciate the night sky. She received a PhD in astronomy from Harvard University, followed by research at the National Radio Astronomy Observatory and as a Hubble Fellow at Johns Hopkins University, where she remains a visiting scholar. She served as the Program Scientist for the Hubble Space Telescope at NASA Headquarters, and she now heads the Laboratory for Exoplanets and Stellar Astrophysics at the NASA Goddard Space Flight Center. She is a Fellow of the American Scientific Affiliation and enjoys speaking to student and church groups on the excitement of seeing God's beauty and ongoing creativity in nature.

Jennifer is married to Mark, a biomedical engineer and jazz percussionist. Together they live with four happy feline friends. Jennifer loves animals of all kinds, exploring nature on foot, boat and bike, and savouring chocolate.

Appendix 7:
Index of Names and Glossary

Augustine – One of the most influential theologians in the Western church. He died in the fifth century AD.

Louis Fieser (1899–1977) – A professor of chemistry who worked on the chemical production of important blood-clotting agents, the use of anti-malarial drugs and the creation of a militarily effective form of napalm.

Stephen Hawking (b. 1944) – The Lucasian Professor of Mathematics at Cambridge University (he plans to retire during 2009). He is known for his work on quantum gravity and black holes and the bestselling popular science book *A Brief History of Time*.

Charles Kingsley (1819–75) – A clergyman in the Church of England, novelist and professor of history. He was a friend of Charles Darwin and one of the first to embrace Darwin's theory of evolution by natural selection. He wrote *Westward Ho!* and *The Water Babies*.

Gottfried Leibniz (1646–1716) – A German polymath known for his contributions to both Mathematics and Philosophy. He is thought to have invented Calculus independently of Isaac Newton and it is his notation, rather than Newton's, which is in common use.

Oskar Schindler (1908–74) – A German industrialist who, at great personal risk, spent his fortune during World War II bribing Nazi officials to protect his Jewish workers.

altruism – Unselfish concern for others (which may involve self-sacrificial acts).

Anthropic Principle – The idea that the universe has been finely tuned to allow for the existence of life.

antimatter – Has the same physical properties as matter (e.g., mass) but the opposite electrical charge. For example, the antimatter equivalent of an electron is a 'positron', which has positive electric charge. When matter and antimatter come together they annihilate, giving out a lot of energy in the process.

astrophysicist – A scientist who uses the laws and theories of physics to study stars and other celestial objects.

atheist – Someone who believes that no gods exist.

automata – Machines that direct themselves according to pre-programmed instructions.

bacterial flagellum – A long 'tail' that bacteria use to propel themselves around, rather like an outboard motor.

Big Bang – The Big Bang was the beginning of the expansion of the universe from its initial hot, dense state, and it's still proceeding (the expansion is actually accelerating). Space is expanding at the same rate in all directions.

biochemistry – The study of the chemistry of living things.

bottom-up – The effect that the 'building blocks' of an object have on its overall properties (e.g., bricks make a strong house).

British Meteorological Office – Officially known as the Met Office, it is the UK's national weather service.

Cambrian – A geologists' term for the period of time from about 542 to 488 million years ago, during which there was a large increase in biological diversity in the fossil record.

camera eye – The type of eye that humans and many other animals have. It works in a similar way to a camera, including a lens, iris and detector.

caveat – A warning or exception.

cell – The unit that makes up a living thing. Animal cells consist of a membrane enclosing whatever parts that particular type of cell needs to do its job. A fat cell contains fat, a bone cell contains a hard substance, a red blood cell contains a substance that carries oxygen around the body, and the long spindly nerve cells are able to pass electrical signals along their length.

chromosome – Each DNA strand in a living cell is wound up tightly into a chromosome. Depending on how human chromosomes are visualized in the lab, they can sometimes look like 'x' shapes or pairs of stripy socks.

climate change – A significant and long-term change in the weather patterns of the planet.

cloning – Scientific definition: Creating a genetically identical copy of a living organism by replacing the nucleus of an unfertilized egg cell with the nucleus of an adult cell (see Session 3 for diagram). Popular definition: Creating an identical being.

cognitive ability – The ability to think and experience things.

constants (physical) – Numbers that are important to the scientific understanding of physical and chemical processes which have been discovered through experiment. There seems to be no obvious reason why they should be that way, but in this universe they just are (e.g., an electron always has the same charge).

convergence – see **evolutionary convergence**

cosmology – The study of the origin, development and overall shape and nature of the universe.

cosmologist – Someone who scientifically studies the origin, development and overall shape and nature of the universe.

dark energy – A hypothetical energy associated with the fabric of space, which increases the expansion of the universe.

dark matter – Hypothetical matter which makes up around 22% of the mass of the universe. Dark matter is thought to have mass but no electric charge, making it very difficult to detect. The nature of this matter is disputed: some say it is made up of massive subatomic particles.

deism – The belief in a supreme being which created the universe but has not been involved in it since then.

DNA – The chemical molecule inside every cell of every living thing that carries the instructions for its growth and development.

early church fathers – The theologians at the beginning of Christianity who had a hand in formalizing the doctrines implied in Scripture.

elements (chemical) – The basic building blocks of everything on earth. The elements include hydrogen, helium, oxygen, carbon and beryllium.

emergence – The idea that complex structures have properties that you couldn't predict if you looked at their individual parts.

empirical – Observed or based on experiment.

epiphenomena – An effect which arises from a process; a side-effect.

evolution – Often used to simply mean change over time. Evolutionary theory in biology refers to the change over huge periods of time of living things that eventually results in new species.

evolutionary convergence – The idea that, because of conditions in the natural world (see constants and Anthropic Principle), evolutionary processes find similar solutions to similar problems, and certain characteristics of living things have evolved many times independently of each other.

Evolutionary Creationism – see **Theistic Evolution**

fall, the – The account of how people became disobedient to God.

fideistic – Something that is based solely on faith or revelation, ignoring reason or intellect.

fine-tuning (see also **Anthropic Principle)** – The idea that the physical constants of the universe are set at the precise values necessary for the existence of biological life.

genetics – The study of inherited characteristics and the variation of inherited characteristics among populations.

geologist – A person who studies the physical structure and history of the earth.

germ cells – Eggs and sperm.

Gluon – see **The Quark and the Gluon**

God of the gaps – An argument which says that when we can't explain something in nature scientifically, that is proof that God exists.

The God Spot – The place (or network of places) that is active in the brain when someone is having a religious experience. Some reductionists say that this religious experience is simply a side effect of other processes in the brain that *makes* someone feel that God exists.

Human Genome Project – The international project to 'read' the whole of the human DNA code (the genome).

inorganic molecules – Molecules which do not contain carbon. Plants turn carbon dioxide (CO_2) into organic molecules, and all organisms are capable of mixing these with 'inorganic' elements to make new 'organic' molecules.

Intelligent Design – The idea that some parts of living things are too complex to have evolved, coupled with the idea that the information contained in DNA cannot have arisen by a process describable in purely material terms, so providing evidence for 'design'.

irreducibly complex – Something which could not have evolved from simpler precursors (in Intelligent Design).

Jurassic – A geologists' term for the period of time between about 199 and 145 million years ago.

laws of nature – Descriptions of the way things behave in nature (e.g., Boyle's law describes the behaviour of gases under certain conditions).

malignant – Bad or harmful, often used with regards to cancer; the opposite of benign (harmless).

materialist – Someone who believes that nothing exists, or is important, except the material world.

metaphysic – Any particular way of interpreting the world.

metaphysical – Impossible to test by experiment. Philosophical or abstract questions.

methodological reductionism – Studying an object by breaking it down and looking at its parts.

molecular biology – The study of biology at a molecular level, especially DNA and the cellular machinery that makes proteins.

multiverse theory – The idea that there are multiple universes. Some people use this to argue that if there are many universes, it's not so surprising that one of them is 'fine-tuned' for life.

multicellular – An organism made up of more than one cell. (Bacteria are 'unicellular'.)

mutation – A change in the DNA code that happens during the life cycle of a living thing. Mutations can be caused by a toxic chemical or other environmental disturbance, or by a mistake in copying the DNA when new cells are made.

NASA – The National Aeronautics and Space Administration, an agency of the US government responsible for the US space program.

naturalistic – Something explained with reference to the natural world only, with no allowance for a supernatural explanation.

Near East, the – A term archaeologists and historians use for the Middle East.

neural correlate – The physical state of the brain associated with a mental state or thought.

neurons – The 'nerve cells' that carry messages in the nervous system and the brain.

neuroscience – The study of the brain and nervous system.

nihilism – Lack of belief in the existence of morality or meaning in life.

order of magnitude – Most commonly used to mean ten times larger (e.g., 5,000 is two orders of magnitude larger than 50).

palaeontologist – Someone who studies fossils.

parallel universes – Other universes that exist at the same time as the one we see (this is important for some forms of multiverse theory).

particle physics – The study of the tiny particles that make up atoms.

preimplantation genetic diagnosis – DNA testing of IVF embryos.

quantum mechanics – The principles underlying the fundamental laws of physics, such as the dual wave-like and particle-like behaviour of matter and radiation.

The Quark and the Gluon – Subatomic particles. Gluons are particles thought to bind quarks together to form larger particles such as protons and neutrons.

radiometric dating – If you measure the amount of a specific radioactive chemical (isotope) present in something, you can measure its age based on two things: 1. The half-life of that radioactive chemical: after a specific amount of time (the half-life), half of the original radioactive isotope atoms will have broken down into other elements. 2. The amount of the isotope which would have been present when the object was formed. It is possible to calculate this through other means. So if you know how much of a certain isotope is left in the sample, you can calculate how old it is.

reductionist – Someone who thinks that you can explain anything by reducing it to its most basic physical properties.

resonance [in the origin of carbon] – Several more basic atomic building blocks can react together to form a new element. If the combined energy of the nuclei which are crashing together is just greater than the resonance level (or nuclear energy level) of the resulting nucleus, the reaction is more efficient. It is this effect that made it possible for carbon to be formed.

Schrödinger equation – An equation which describes the behaviour of the tiny particles that make up atoms. It describes how a quantity called the wave function changes with time. The probability that a measurement gives a particular result is derived from the wave function.

sedimentary rock – Rock formed by laying down and compressing layers of sediment (dust, ash, sand, etc.).

somatic cells – All the cells in the body except eggs and sperm.

special relativity – Einstein's theory about space and time: the speed of light in a vacuum is the same for all observers.

tectonic plates – Rigid structures which make up the earth's outer crust. They float on top of a layer of magma (molten rock). They separate, collide and rub against each other causing volcanoes, earthquakes and tsunamis. They also allow nutrients, minerals and gases from the interior of the earth out onto the surface and into the atmosphere.

theism – Belief in a personal God who created the world and who also sustains and continues to be involved in it.

Theistic Evolution (or Evolutionary Creationism) – The belief that God created life through the process of evolution.

top-down – The effect an object or whole has on the parts of which it is made.

transhumanism – The idea of enhancing human abilities with technology in extreme ways.

vertebrates – Animals with a spinal cord: amphibians, birds, fish, mammals and reptiles.

Young Earth Creationism – The belief that Genesis should be interpreted as a literal, historical and scientific account, and therefore that God created the world between 6,000 and 10,000 years ago in six twenty-four hour days.

Endnotes

i. Deborah helped to write parts of Sessions 2 and 1b, particularly the Briefing Sheets: The Big Bang and Views on Genesis 1.

ii. Figures from **http://esa.un.org/unpp**.

iii. From Peter Saunders, 'The Bible and Medical Ethics' (Word Alive 1998 lecture series), **www.cmf.org.uk/ethics/word_alive_98_lecture_3.htm**.

iv. **www.abc.net.au/rn/allinthemind/stories/2006/1698423.htm**.

v. Examples and scenario taken with permission from a paper by D. Alexander called 'Cloning Humans: Distorting the Image of God?' (The Cambridge Papers 10.2 [June 2001]; **www.jubilee-centre.org**, Jubilee House, 3 Hooper Street, Cambridge, CB1 2NZ).

vi. Extract with permission from D. Alexander and R.S. White, Beyond Belief: Science, Faith and Ethical Challenges (Lion, 2004), pp. 152–3.

vii. Copied, with permission from Life in Our Hands: A Christian Perspective on Genetics and Cloning, John Bryant and John Searle, IVP, 2004, page 152.

viii. 'GM' in this case refers to 'Somatic' gene therapy – a treatment that affects a tissue or tissues in the body, but not the eggs or sperm, so that the treatment does not affect the next generation (because that raises a host of other issues and is illegal in the UK).

ix. See note above.

Test of FAITH

THE BOOK: SPIRITUAL JOURNEYS WITH SCIENTISTS

The book **Test of FAITH: Spiritual Journeys with Scientists** tells the stories of ten scientists featured in the '**Test of FAITH**' video materials. These respected physicists, biologists and brain scientists share their life stories and their reflections on science and faith.

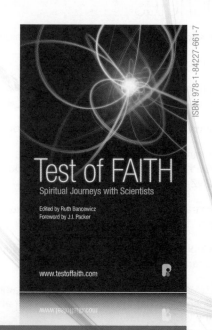

ISBN: 978-1-84227-661-7

The contributors are:

Dr Francis Collins, Professor Alister McGrath, Dr Ard Louis, Dr Jennifer Wiseman, Professor Bill Newsome, Rev Dr John Polkinghorne, Rev Dr Alasdair Coles, Dr Deborah B Haarsma, Professor Rosalind Picard, and **Professor John Bryant.**

www.testoffaith.com

Resources for churches from the **Faraday Institute for Science and Religion**

A range of resources designed to help you explore **science-faith issues**

- VIDEOS
- ARTICLES
- STORIES
- REVIEWS
- MATERIALS FOR CHURCH SERVICES
- EXTRA RESOURCES TO ACCOMPANY THE **TEST OF FAITH** COURSE
- RESOURCES FOR YOUTH GROUPS

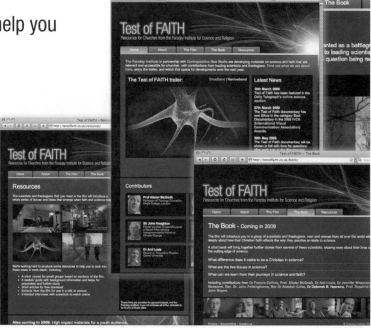

Test of FAITH

Youth materials

HAS SCIENCE DISPROVED GOD? HOW WAS THE WORLD CREATED? WHAT MAKES ME UNIQUE?

These are hot topics for many young people. For those wanting to tackle these subjects with their young people it can be intimidating to know what to do, where to turn, what answers would be required and which would be ridiculed.

The **Test of Faith** team have developed resources for **11-14** and **11-18 year olds** that are designed to meet that need. They will equip youth workers not necessarily with lots of answers to apologetic questions, but rather with an appreciation of the debate, the range of questions being asked, and the way in which answers can be explored.

The **14-18s** sessions make use of the documentary **Test of FAITH**.

Available free on **www.testoffaith.com** from **Autumn 2009**

Test of FAITH

Resources for schools

Covering topics found in many **GCSE** and **A Level RE** curricula such as **creationism**, **evolution**, **origins of the universe** and **the problems of evil and suffering**, the resources for schools are based on the **three part documentary Test of FAITH**.

The topics are covered through five sessions, entitled:
- THE MYTH OF CONFLICT
- FILLING THE GAPS
- HOW DID LIFE DEVELOP?
- EVIL AND SUFFERING
- FREEWILL AND DETERMINISM

Available on **www.stapleford-centre.org** from **August 2009**

The resources unpack the issues surrounding these areas with differentiated materials suitable for use with pupils **14-18** years old. **Background information**, a **glossary** and a **bibliography** are included to support teachers in delivery of this part of the syllabus. Links are given to **GCSE** and **A Level** syllabi.